CHRISTIAN PERSPECTIVES ON
THE FINANCIAL CRASH

Christian Perspectives on the Financial Crash

ST PAULS

ST PAULS Publishing
187 Battersea Bridge Road, London SW11 3AS, UK
www.stpaulspublishing.com

Copyright © ST PAULS UK, 2010
ISBN 978-0-85439-767–9

A catalogue record is available for this book from the British Library.

Set by Tukan DTP, Stubbington, Fareham, UK
Printed by Società San Paolo, Alba (Cn), Italy

ST PAULS is an activity of the priests and brothers
of the Society of St Paul who proclaim the Gospel
through the media of social communication.

CONTENTS / AUTHORS

INTRODUCTION

THE MOST REVD VINCENT NICHOLS
Archbishop of Westminster

———

WIDER LESSONS FROM THE FINANCIAL CRASH[1]

In the aftermath of the recent financial crash, we often heard the phrase: 'We are living in exceptional times.' Indeed it became one of the Prime Minister's most quoted remarks, and it is true that the upheaval in the world's financial systems and the loss of confidence it produced led to effects that are having an impact on all of us: job losses, companies closing down, building sites standing silent are now evident every day.

Christians should ask God's blessing on their endeavours, especially in public service. We should ask Him to give us some insight into our situation, in the light of the truth about our human nature. We should ask ourselves what we learned about ourselves and our society while living in a time of plenty and also what we can learn about ourselves in a time of austerity and hardship.

Many have commented that the root causes of the financial crisis are ethical. Indeed the very term 'credit' comes from '*credere*' and indicates that trust and belief are central. Commentators point out that the financial systems, while closely regulated, were lacking in clear ethical foundations. It can be put like this: a market controlled only by regulation, sooner or later, will succumb to its inherent drive for profit at all costs. Of course the profit motive is crucial; of course responsibility to investors is a significant balancing factor in risk taking. But what we have seen is that, left to itself, the financial market has no robust external frame of reference, not even a wider economic framework. It has behaved as if it exists for itself and within itself and to the benefit of those who are part of it. What the market lacked was the perspective and practice of true virtue, which builds trust and without which every human endeavour is unstable.

7

Perhaps the same can be said of our society at large. We have neglected the development of shared ethical values and principles to guide and shape our behaviour, believing that to be an unattainable goal, and we have substituted raft after raft of regulation. Yet a society controlled only by regulation succumbs, sooner or later, to our inherent drive for self-interest. Society too needs the perspective and practice of true virtue.

The word 'virtue' is not one we use too often in public discourse. Indeed in general we confine such ethical talk to the private sphere. In the public domain we are hesitant to ask for more than compliance with the rules, although we do now talk more about the values which we need to promote across society, particularly those of respect and tolerance. Yet this notion of 'values' is a flexible and friendly one: I can establish or negotiate my own values, and they tend to accommodate to my own behaviour. But talk of virtues is more demanding, for a virtue is more like a hard-earned skill such as those used in the performance of music or sport. Of course, in such a performance the rules have to be observed. But the rules of the game alone have never produced a masterful performance. Only dedication, sacrifice and true skill do that. This is the arena of virtue.

The Christian faith is a guardian of true human virtues. Traditionally a virtue is expressed as being 'personal capacity for action, the fruit of a series of good actions, a power for progress and perfection'. If we take, for example, the good shepherd from the first reading of the Catholic feast of Christ the King, he is a virtuous man. He knows that his task is to care for the sheep, whatever their condition. The necessary virtues have been his practice; they are his true capacity; they contribute to progress and the wider good. He is vigilant and responsive, not to the cause of his own well-being but to that of the sheep. He will 'keep them in view', 'rescue them', 'pasture them', showing them where to rest, bringing back the stray, bandaging the wounded, watching over 'the fat and healthy'. With his effort, progress is made in the wellbeing of all. This is the fruit of virtue.

The human virtues guarded by the Church, but of course not by the Church alone but by other faiths and many others of goodwill, are those of prudence, courage, justice and temperance.

Prudence is the virtue by which we discern the true good in every circumstance, and the right way to achieve it. It is the opposite of rashness and carelessness. It is needed in an age of advanced technology when the presumption is that if something can be done then it should be done.

Courage is the virtue that ensures firmness in difficulties, enabling us to conquer our fear, even fear of death, and face up to hardship. It is the opposite of opportunism and evasiveness. It is needed in an age of pragmatism and cautious self-protection. Courage produces heroism.

Justice is the constant and firm will to give one's due to God and to our neighbours, be they near or far. Justice towards God is the 'virtue of religion'; towards our neighbours it is the respecting of their rights and the fulfilling of my duties, promoting equality and the common good. It is the opposite of self-centredness and unrestricted profiteering. Justice towards God is needed in an age of public secularism and justice to our neighbour in an age of globalisation.

Temperance is the virtue that moderates the attraction of pleasures and provides balance in the use of created goods. It is the opposite of greed and self-indulgence. It is needed in an age of consumerism and excess.

We are in need of the practice of these virtues at all times. In times of plenty they promote generosity and philanthropy, good working practices in every enterprise and the service not just of one's own benefit but of the common good of all. In times of austerity they lead us to a simpler life-style, to a practical relief of material poverty, to a discovery of a sense of deeper shared identity and mutual concern, to wise practical judgements about what is of lasting importance and what simply the fruit of excess.

The exercise of these virtues will make good shepherds of us all especially for those hit hardest by the effects of the financial crash. May I add that these human virtues have their true foundation in the greater, theological virtues: faith hope and love, which bind us to God and to each other.

The Gospel reading of the feast of Christ the King also helps us in our quest to understand life in society. It affirms an ancient and unchanging truth: there is a judgement still to come. You can easily recall the scene depicted in the Gospel, and so often painted on the archways of churches: the Last Judgement, with the virtuous on one hand, the selfish and foolish on the other. In mediaeval paintings there was always a bishop among the condemned. Quite often there was one on the other side, too, as if the artist was hedging his bets! But we need to listen carefully. The criterion by which the judgement is given is quite simple: have we been merciful? Have we responded to those caught in poverty, misfortune or in the consequences of their own behaviour? If we seek the mercy of God for ourselves, then the question we are asked is: have we extended that mercy to others?

Mercy is simply understood: it is the virtue by which the application of expected rules is suspended, out of love and compassion. Mercy, like all the virtues, gets us beyond the regulations and into the true heart of our condition. Mercy enables us to start again, to make progress after failure, to receive what we don't deserve. A family or society that is incapable of showing mercy to its weak and vulnerable is dead from within. The wooden application of regulation squeezes the life out of us, and can be rescued or redeemed only by lives of true virtue and above all by mercy, the most precious quality of God and the one in which we rejoice today.

The vision of St Paul is that of the fulfilling of all things, all things on this earth and all things in heaven, in the final resurrection. Christ is the instigator and the first fruit of this fulfilment. In him, whom we proclaim as King, we get a glimpse of our true destiny. This is the end for which we work, accepting the call to perfection while knowing, that left to ourselves, it is beyond our achievement. But, united in a common humanity, filled by the grace of God which comes through Christ, we can do so much.

Of course the economics must be right and we must pray for those whose responsibility this is. The insights of the Christian-economist authors of this book should help to inform wider discussion of the economic matters surrounding the financial crash. But whatever the economic policies adopted in response to the crash, we also need to ensure that we work together in the right spirit: an effort that must be shaped by the exercise of true human virtues and inspired by the Holy Spirit of our loving and merciful God, Father of all, in whom all things will come to their fulfilment.

NOTE

1   This chapter is adapted from my homily on the feast of Christ the King, given on 23 November 2008 in the Metropolitan Cathedral of St Chad, Birmingham.

DIFFERING VIEWS ON
THE CAUSES OF THE CRASH[1]

PHILIP BOOTH

Professor of Insurance and Risk Management, Cass Business School; Editorial and Programme Director, Institute of Economic Affairs.

INTRODUCTION

Most major catastrophic events require the interaction of several causes to create what is sometimes known as a 'perfect storm'. Economists still today, seventy years after the event, argue about the causes of the 'roaring twenties' and subsequent Great Depression. As with the recent financial crash, many at the time of the Great Depression blamed unbridled capitalism and greed. Subsequent reflection and study has suggested that incompetent – or at least severely misguided – monetary policy was at least partly, if not largely, to blame.

There are also upstream and downstream causes of problems in all walks of life. It may be the case, for example, that banks created all sorts of complex financial products which led to serious problems in the financial system, but it is still important to ask the question, 'Why did they do that?' Their activities may have been highly distorted by regulation, tax systems or other factors. Similarly, if we think of human greed as being a significant cause of the crash then, given the persistence of greed in all societies, it is worthwhile asking why human greed had such serious consequences in the particular context of the banking system in the period 2007-2008. It is important to untangle obvious causes of the crash from causes that may be less obvious but potentially more important.

This chapter does not attempt to moralise. It is an attempt to describe, for the Christian non-economist, the various economic malfunctions that led to the financial crash of 2008 in order to provide perspective for the later chapters that deal more explicitly with issues of direct concern to Christians.

THE ROLE OF MONETARY POLICY

It is now widely accepted that the boom and bust of the 1920s and 1930s, culminating in the Great Depression, arose to a large degree as a result of catastrophically mismanaged monetary policy. The same is true of the Japanese boom, bust and malaise of the late twentieth century. So it is natural that we should start by examining monetary policy to see if it turns out to be a major cause of the crash of 2008. As we shall see, so it turns out to be: loose monetary policy in the USA over an extended period of time, and in the UK over a shorter period of time, led to a financial bubble.

But what do we mean by 'loose monetary policy' and how does it happen? Central banks, such as the Federal Reserve in the USA and the Bank of England in the UK, set interest rates to achieve various objectives. In the UK, the Bank of England is supposed to set the level of interest rates at which banks can borrow from the central bank in order to ensure that the economy stays on track to meet a particular target for inflation.[2] This level of interest rates forms a 'base rate' above which other interest rates – including mortgage rates – tend to be set.

If interest rates are held too low for too long, consumption and investment tends to rise as people borrow more and savings tend to fall. This is precisely what happened in the early twenty-first century – especially in the USA.

Loose monetary policy of this type is a major cause of high inflation. In this case, though, consumer price inflation (the prices of goods we buy in the shops) was relatively subdued, partly because of globalisation and the falls in prices of imported consumer products. Instead, money poured into asset markets – houses, shares, credit instruments and so on. The higher asset prices that resulted raised the value of collateral against secured loans such as mortgages. That encouraged people to borrow more against their house values, for example by equity release and, because the values of assets were higher, lenders thought that their lending was secure.

Loose monetary policy led people to borrow more than they could really afford to repay because interest rates were held below the level at which they should have been set. The boom in house prices also turned sour. This meant that, in the US especially, borrowers could not repay their loans – the so-called sub-prime mortgage crisis. Banks then made huge losses on these loans, many of which were hidden away in complex securities that had been traded and bought by banks in many countries, including the UK.

There are many sub-plots. Loans were not monitored very effectively because of the complex securities that were created and traded. There was dishonesty and sharp practice by both borrowers and lenders. Some of these sub-plots are discussed in other chapters.

In many senses loose monetary policy seriously distorted the behaviour of participants in financial markets. But, even if such monetary policy mistakes are an important primary cause of the financial crash, we would probably prefer a financial system that is able to withstand the effects of errors that will be made, from time to time, by central bankers. Mistakes in the conduct of monetary policy will always happen. Central bankers are not omniscient. We therefore need financial markets that are robust in the face of monetary policy mistakes.

RECKLESS BANKERS AND RECKLESS CUSTOMERS

The red herring of hedge funds

Were actors within financial markets at all culpable? Or was the crash simply a symptom of failure of monetary policy (see above) and regulation (see below) whilst participants in financial markets behaved like angels? Of course, this is not the case. But, first, we should deal with a red-herring. Some have put the blame for the financial crisis on short sellers, such as hedge funds, who, it is argued, increased financial market volatility and helped to bring down the banks. Christians have made such comments, including one very high-profile comment by the Archbishop of York who compared short sellers with robber barons in a speech to City bankers in

September 2008. The EU has reacted to such views by proposing more regulation of these institutions.

There are many legitimate debates about the crash – debates that divide the left from believers in free, relatively unregulated, financial markets. However, the position that short selling brought down banks that were otherwise sound is one for which there is really very little evidence indeed.[3]

When investors reduce a 'long' position in a particular share (say in HSBC) they sell shares that they own. Taking a short position involves selling a share (again, say, in HSBC) that an investor does not own. Normally, the share would be 'borrowed' from another investor and sold. We generally sell shares that we own when we expect their price to fall relative to the prices of other shares. Investors such as hedge funds sell shares that they *do not* own in the hope of buying them back (as they must to give them back to the party from which they have borrowed them) at a lower price. The motivation is the same whether an investor reduces a long position in a particular share or takes a short position by selling shares that it has borrowed: the investor is hoping to profit from a fall in the share price.

There is, in fact, no inherent difference in terms of the effect on financial markets between reducing a long position and short-selling a security. Furthermore, there is simply no evidence that short-selling activity had anything to do with bringing down the banks. In the crucial days before the fall of HBOS, to which many of the critics of short selling referred, shorting activity in its shares seemed, if anything, to have decreased somewhat. Indeed, Professor of Finance at Cardiff Business School, Laurence Copeland, argues that one of the problems before the crash was that financial institutions were not sufficiently active in selling and short selling the shares of banks. Banks had made very bad decisions, argues Copeland. The job of shareholders and other investors is to monitor the management of banks and other companies. If shares are over-valued, both ordinary selling and short-selling lead to a fall in share price. This sends a signal to the market that the management is doing a bad job. Directors should take note and take action to improve performance. Instead, problems were allowed to fester.

Moving away from banking 'Captain Mainwaring' style

Some also argue that banks have made big mistakes by departing from the traditional model of banking. Dembinski (2009) makes this case powerfully in a book which is rooted in Christian social thinking. In recent years banks have tended to offer loans and fund them not through savers' deposits but through a process known as securitisation. This is a complex process. Banks create and sell securities to investors such as other banks, pension funds, hedge funds and so on. The interest payments on these securities are met by the interest payments the banks themselves receive on the loans they have made. This means that banks have less concern for 'relationships' with customers and might not properly monitor those who borrow from them. If a customer defaults on a loan, it does not affect the bank that makes the loan because the loan has been sold on to another investor. Of course, if banks sell securities backed by lousy loans into the market investors will not buy them. However, risky loans have often been bundled into complex securities and the risk of those loans has been obscured and measured by complex models built on assumptions which may have been naïve. Dembinski argues that in this whole process 'transactions' (the buying and selling of securities) have become more important than relationships (a direct relationship between a bank and a borrower).

As part of this evolution of banking, just as banks have sold on loans that they have made to customers, they have bought such loans sold by other banks. Many of the UK banks that have suffered huge losses did so because they bought portfolios of loans backed by mortgages made to US homebuyers. Again, the risks were obscured and not properly measured.

There is something to be said for the thesis that this process was an important contributor to the crash and Catherine Cowley discusses such issues in the next chapter. But, at the same time, it should not be felt that this new model of banking was simply developed by people who had an eye only on short-term profits and fee generation. It is possible that incentives were distorted in some institutions and that this led some executives within banks to create new products simply to earn fees. It is also possible that securitisation was pursued to try to reduce the impact of certain types of regulation. However, there were many positive reasons why banks got involved in the process of securitisation. Non-bank investors, such as pension funds, unit trusts and mutual funds, have increasingly wanted to invest in more secure investment instruments and – despite the apparent risk of some securitised bonds – these instruments provided investors with reasonable security and a return greater than that from bank deposits or government bonds. In turn this whole process allowed borrowers to obtain mortgages at lower interest rates. Securitised loans also allowed banks to diversify and seemed to spread risk around the financial system.

This is not simply an ex-post justification for unjustifiable behaviour. Central bankers and government regulators supported the process too. Paul Tucker, recently promoted to Deputy Governor of the Bank of England, said in a speech as late as April 2007: 'So it would seem that there is a good deal to welcome in the greater dispersion of risk made possible by modern instruments, markets and institutions.'[4] It is also notable that a large proportion of the losses in the banking system were the result of the activity of the US-government-backed mortgage securitisation warehouses of Fannie Mae and Freddie Mac. These were not creations of the market economy. Some, such as Dembinksi, would argue that the whole financial system has been distorted by greed and the dominance of transactions over relationships and that this has even infected government regulators. However, it is also possible that well-meaning people simply made errors of judgement. Indeed, they may even have made decisions that were correct given the information that they had available to them at the time. It is true that many people working for banks and many senior executives could have been caught up in the euphoria when they should have taken a step back and taken their responsibilities more seriously. However, we should be careful before we issue wholesale condemnations of those involved in financial markets. Human imperfection does not only manifest itself in the form of explicit sinfulness and outright reckless greed, but also in the form of neglect or even well-meaning failure.

Facing up to responsibilities

Nevertheless, we should ask serious questions of participants in financial markets. Directors should ensure that a business is managed in order to create value for its owners, yet banks have collapsed. Creating value for owners is not the same as focusing on 'short-term profit' as some have suggested[5]. A director is answerable to shareholders and shareholders require the long-term continuation of a successful business model. It is legitimate for banks' directors to be asked a number of questions, including but not limited to the following: were they taking proper responsibility for understanding the risks of the business and ensuring that these risks were properly managed? Did they ensure that the reward packages of senior management properly aligned managers' incentives with the long-term success of the business? Did directors allow the business to be captured by senior management? If directors fail to hold management to account and do not stand up to senior management if it is necessary to do so, then they abrogate their responsibilities.

Similarly, senior management must ask whether they were behaving ethically too. Sales targets for employees that can be achieved only by employees selling products they know to be unsuitable; the pursuit of transaction fees by underwriting business or pursuing acquisitions that are not properly priced and the risks of which are not properly assessed; not properly monitoring risks; and so on are all symptoms of a management culture that puts maximising rewards for current managers first and the long-term health of the business second.

Nevertheless, we still must ask why banks, and the system as a whole, were so vulnerable to these problems. Poor or lazy behaviour can arise in any business but it does not normally lead to the complete implosion of a large part of a whole sector of the economy.

At lower levels too, people should ask themselves about their conduct. Trust and prudence is essential amongst both borrowers and lenders alike – this includes those in a bank responsible for the most minor lending decisions. It is clear that junior managers in banks were motivated, at least to some extent, by lending targets and paid insufficient attention to the ability of borrowers to repay debts. It is also clear that, especially in the US where most of the losses in the mortgage market have been concentrated, borrowers lied on mortgage proposal forms.

Some argue that regulation can help promote a more orderly market. However, it can also be argued that increased statutory regulatory responsibility in financial markets has led to a situation where the importance of more ethical and honest relationships has been crowded out and, in fact, compliance with regulation has displaced trust. Archbishop Vincent Nichols has a mature reflection on this subject in the introduction to this book. No amount of additional regulation can substitute for a decline in ethical standards.

THE REGULATORY MORASS

Careless regulation

It is impossible to determine whether more ethical behaviour would have prevented the crash from happening. The crash may have simply manifested itself in a different way given other things that were happening in the wider economy. However, it is also the case that many of the loans that led to losses should never have been made by banks in the first place. As we have noted, loose monetary policy and low interest rates might have encouraged too much borrowing. This may have been reinforced by greed and understandable – if misguided – attempts to get onto the housing ladder by people who could not really afford to do so. But, in the process of granting loans to those who could not afford to repay them, other factors were at work too.

The US federal government passed legislation that made illegal the practice of banks refusing loans on the ground that people were buying homes in poor areas with high unemployment.[6] This legislation was gradually tightened and backed up by regulation at state level. Very high levels of damages could be imposed on banks that were regarded as failing to comply with these rules. The two huge state-sponsored mortgage warehouses, Fannie Mae and Freddie Mac, were both able to provide lower cost loans to households which were poor risks because of their government guarantees and they also had explicit targets for lending to the poor. The US government Housing and Urban Development Corporation gave these institutions a target of 42% of mortgage financing to people on below median income in 1996. This target was extended to 50% in 2000 and 52% in 2005.

The consequences were disastrous. The banking crisis which led to the financial crash would certainly have been much less serious if it were not for lending to what are known as 'sub-prime' risks in the US mortgage market. This lending was explicitly encouraged by regulation and also implicitly encouraged by the presence of Fannie Mae and Freddie Mac backed by the US federal government.

Deregulation or re-regulation?

Some economists have criticised the process of 'deregulation' of the banking sector which, they argue, has allowed the banking system to take greater risks and operate with greater freedom. In particular, what some describe as the 'casino' part of the bank – investment banking – has often been undertaken in the same businesses as the 'utility banking' on which we depend directly for our current accounts. It is argued that the operation of casinos has brought down utilities. The Royal Bank of Scotland, for example, might have made losses on its general high street lending and savings businesses, but these losses would not have led to the virtual insolvency of the bank – the serious losses were made in the more speculative areas. Historically, the division between investment banking and retail banking in the USA was mandated by the Glass-Steagall

Act, passed after the Wall Street Crash and during the Great Depression. However, this was repealed in 1999.

There are several nuances to this line of argument. Firstly, many models of regulation have existed in different countries in the last 150 years and the legal separation of investment from retail banking is not a standard approach that has been adopted widely. There is no evidence that legal separation has made banking systems more stable. Also, US retail banks made serious mistakes in their retail operations by lending to poor, sub-prime risks and this would have happened even if investment banks and retail banks had not been joined together.[7]

Regarding the deregulation argument more generally, it is probably true to say that banks are permitted to undertake a wider range of activities than they were for most of the twentieth century – though financial markets were extraordinarily free in the UK in the nineteenth century, as well as being highly sophisticated. However, the detailed way in which those activities are undertaken is now regulated in incredible detail in a way which nobody would have anticipated happening thirty years ago. The Financial Services Authority in the UK has the most remarkable 'Prudential Regulation' manual which is simply mind-boggling in its detail. Furthermore, regulation comes from international sources via the European Union and the Basel Capital Accord.

The worst of all worlds

It is possible that the particular form of financial market regulation that we have has made matters worse and not better. It may be overstating the point to argue that the crash was caused by regulatory failure, but it certainly appears that there is nothing that regulators did that made the crash less likely or made its consequences less dire. International banking regulation encouraged the creation of the new opaque financial instruments described above and in later chapters. Because gearing[8] and capital[9] are regulated, banks find more and more opaque ways to obtain the effect of gearing without doing the things that regulators penalise. Thus they create complex financial instruments and structures that few within, never mind outside, the industry understand. Risk taking was therefore harder for shareholders to monitor and penalise. Furthermore, regulators encouraged financial institutions to use similar quantitative risk models for setting their capital and assessing risks. It is quite possible that these models were flawed. Certainly they seemed unable to assess extreme risks effectively.

This all led to several serious consequences. For example, if the risk models that regulators encouraged banks to use were to go wrong for one financial institution, then they were likely to go wrong for them all – at the same time. The models also encouraged financial institutions to take similar risks and the risks were generally assessed using historical data. This meant that institutions would react in similar ways when things went wrong leading to consequences that would not be captured by the models. In particular, when institutions became distressed they all rushed for the exit, leading to 'fire sales' and illiquidity. Conceptual thinking about risk was discouraged and complexity was encouraged by the regulatory emphasis on complex modelling. Those who should have been monitoring banks (such as shareholders) were reassured that risk was being kept in bounds, even though the extent of the risks they were taking could not be understood at a conceptual level: knowledge replaced understanding.

Regulation also created fundamentally disordered processes within financial institutions. Instead of releasing information to the market, the management of financial institutions had their most important relationships with regulators. Interestingly, the least regulated financial institutions, it appears, were those that bore least responsibility for and were least affected by the crash.

We perhaps have too much confidence in regulatory agencies to "perfect" the financial system – as has been argued by Archbishop Nichols in the introduction. Just as some have argued that there were distorted incentives within banks caused, for example, by high bonuses and limited liability, there are also distorted incentives structurally embedded within regulatory agencies. Often regulators have an incentive to be too cautious and risk averse because they do not want problems to arise on their watch for which they will be held responsible. Paradoxically, once a problem arises, regulators have an incentive to delay action so as not to draw attention to a problem. Firstly, they may hope that an improvement in the markets will make the problem go away. Secondly, many regulators later seek jobs with institutions that they have regulated – they may well not wish to treat such institutions too harshly.

Governments also provided guarantees at several levels and this reduced the incentives for stakeholders to monitor banks. For example, in most countries, deposits are guaranteed. In the nineteenth century, banks in Britain competed with each other to demonstrate how sound they were – now depositors get the benefits of more risk taking through higher interest rates but do not bear the costs of risk taking because of deposit insurance.[10] The bank bailouts, which were widely expected, especially in the USA given past experience, made investors in banks less cautious. In the UK, there was also no easy way to wind up a bank without causing chaos within the whole financial system – so banks had to be rescued at huge expense to the taxpayer. Not being able to wind up an insolvent bank in an orderly fashion has three implications. Firstly, it means that a bank failure is likely to cause chaos – thus the authorities step in and take responsibility. Secondly, the knowledge that this will happen creates moral hazard amongst all who provide capital for the bank and thus makes them less cautious. Finally, it can be regarded as unjust, in a sense, that taxpayers rather than a bank's creditors take responsibility for the losses.

Clearer thinking needed

Economists will debate the appropriate regulatory response to these problems. However, they are generally agreed that it is a recipe for disaster if banks' shareholders, bondholders and depositors all know that they are to be bailed out by government yet they can undertake all activities in an unregulated environment. We can respond to this in at least three ways. One is by regulation that limits the activities of banks: for example, laws could ensure that risky investment banking is done in completely separate organisations from retail banking. Secondly, banks can be allowed to undertake a wide range of activities but those activities can be regulated more tightly. Thirdly, it would also be a reasonable approach to allow banks freedom to operate yet make sure that those who finance banks suffer all the losses when banks fail. The regulatory regime that existed before the crash gave banks relative freedom in many respects without calling banks to account for their mistakes.

TYING UP THE ECONOMICS AND THE ETHICS

How does a focus on economic, policy and regulatory issues fit in with Christian concern about ethical issues? Christians talk about how public policy should be oriented towards the common good – or creating the conditions for human flourishing. Policy decisions can have both an economic and an ethical aspect. An analogy can be drawn with the welfare state. There is at the moment great concern about the effect that the welfare state has on work incentives, marriage and so on – for example, in relation to incapacity benefit and the treatment of couples in the benefit system. These problems also involve ethical aspects. For example, it is wrong for a person to claim incapacity benefit when they are fit for work. In the same way, economic incentives and ethical issues come together in governing behaviour in the financial system. Indeed, analogies between the welfare state and some of the problems in the banking system go further. Somebody might feel that if they tick all the right boxes on the incapacity benefit form and successfully pass the doctor's examination then they should claim the benefit and not worry about looking for work. A more conscientious person may realise that they can, technically, qualify for the benefit but that they should go out looking for work all the same. The same happens in financial institutions. Individuals working within them have often ticked all the right regulatory boxes and not thought about the ethical spirit of their actions: Iain Allan deals with this problem in a later chapter.

Christian commentators on the welfare state, such as Frank Field and Iain Duncan Smith, have pointed out that when welfare systems do not run with the grain of self interest and human nature, disaster is likely to follow. Human nature is such that distorted incentives can actually erode ethical behaviour – except within those who have the very strongest ethical standards.

The argument here is that there have been similar problems in the financial sector. Yes, ethical issues must be given serious consideration. It is certainly true that a market economy without strong ethical norms will not function as efficiently and be as conducive towards promoting the common good. At the same time, however, we should not try to push water uphill. Those who work in financial markets are very sharp and respond to price signals rapidly. We cannot assume that all will have the highest standards of ethical behaviour. As such it is important that, in financial markets, we do not incentivise poor ethical behaviour and that the self interest of participants is aligned with the interests of society as a whole.[11]

The Archbishop of Canterbury famously suggested recently that "economics is too important to be left to economists". This is perhaps not the most helpful way to describe the problem with which we are trying to wrestle. The point is that different disciplines are complementary and overlapping. We can, as a result of a deeper Christian understanding, develop ethical precepts of behaviour that can be applied in financial markets – and elsewhere in society. But economists can also give advice not just on the technical things that go wrong in financial markets but about the sort of structures that might be conducive to encouraging – or at least not discouraging – ethical behaviour.

If greed was at the root of the financial crisis, the obvious question is why was this greed so destructive? Are people greedier now than thirty years ago? Were they greedier in 1929 (at the time of the Wall Street Crash) than in 1959? In a market economy, greed should be naturally restrained because one cannot benefit oneself without providing something of value to somebody else. A business as a whole needs to satisfy customers. In order to ensure that, senior managers have an incentive to monitor junior managers; the board has an incentive to monitor the senior managers; shareholders should monitor the board; and so on. Yet many banks lost between 90% and 100% of their value. Why did greed and the desire to make money actually destroy financial institutions? Why did this happen in banking in the early twenty-first century as opposed to some other time? Why did it happen in banking rather than in micro-chip making?

It is simplistic but perhaps helpful to divide ethical actions within financial markets into two categories. There are certain actions that are always – to Christians and to others – objectively wrong. This will include lying to counterparties. There are other actions where it is easy to articulate ethical principles but where the application of those principles requires a degree of discernment and judgement. An example of this second type of action would be the decision whether or not to strike a deal that created a complex financial product that provided immediate fee income for the bank but which might be of doubtful long-term value to shareholders.

Though the first type of decision would appear to be a wholly ethical one, economists have identified economic aspects of such decisions. For example, in markets where reputation is an important business selling point, ethical behaviour is likely to be reinforced rather than undermined – somebody who is untrustworthy will not get business. Also, there will be some people who are more likely to succumb to temptation than others – people who are weak willed. There is evidence that state regulation can crowd out the need to develop a good reputation as a business selling point.

When markets are distorted in various ways the second type of ethical decision becomes much more difficult to take prudently. A decision that requires discernment in turn requires the prudential consideration of a number of factors. If the flows of information are distorted by government interventions in financial markets, it is very difficult to come to a sound prudential judgement. Does the creation of the complex product help spread risk round the financial system and lower the costs of mortgages to customers or is it simply an expensive device to get round regulatory impositions? It can be very difficult to tell the difference if the wrong regulatory environment exists. We must ensure that regulation does not make ethical judgements more difficult.

Another aspect of the overlap of economic issues with ethical issues relates to the discussion of bankers' bonuses. Some have argued that the level of bonuses that we have seen is unjustified and unethical and that bonus structures lead bankers to take risks. Whether large bonuses are unethical is a moot point and is discussed in the next chapter. But, in thinking about the public policy response, we should consider reasons why high bonuses exist. There is evidence to suggest that high bonuses result from the low likelihood of failure within banks arising from implicit guarantees governments put under the banking system. In other words it is not that large bonuses create incentives to take on risk but the incentives to take on risk (caused by government guarantees) lead to bigger bonuses. If large bonuses are unethical, we should not simply consider that issue on face value: we should also take a step back and consider whether something can be done to reduce the distortions that encourage banks to pay large bonuses. After all, if bonuses were paid for work that increased economic welfare, few would object. If, however, bonuses are paid for inventing products that leave taxpayers with the risks and banks with the profits, then there is something wrong. Sometimes when markets are distorted in subtle ways it is difficult for anybody to know whether particular behaviour genuinely involves wealth creation or simply leads to risks being shunted onto taxpayers. Developing "just" reward packages that reward people for their contribution to the business becomes much more difficult.

OTHER ASPECTS OF HUMAN IMPERFECTION

We would have had a better outcome if the financial system had been populated with good people. But greed and sinfulness are not the only manifestations of human imperfection. We should therefore be careful before wielding blame unnecessarily. Some of the poor decisions made by the US and UK monetary authorities discussed above might have resulted from a lack of 'backbone', but other decisions may simply have been misguided, or shown in retrospect to be in error. Similarly, in banks, no doubt there was unrestrained greed operating in some quarters, but there was also a great deal of simple human error. Many independent analysts (and regulators) genuinely felt that innovations reduced risk. Perhaps those market analysts and regulators were lazy and did not want to challenge the consensus in the market – but, more likely, they simply made misjudgements.

As Christians, we should try to make the world a better place by being better people. We should examine how we behave as consumers (do we consume too much, have too much debt and save too little?); as bankers (do we 'hard sell' inappropriate products?); as directors (do we challenge the management and come out of our comfort zone?); and so on. We should do this without questioning whether specific good will come from ethically correct actions – though no doubt it will. But, nevertheless, in an imperfect world, many honest mistakes will also be made and some of those mistakes will have catastrophic effects.

Ethical behaviour should always be pursued for its own sake. However, it will also make the financial world a better place; it will contribute to the common good; it will create an atmosphere of trust and harmony; and it will make financial institutions better institutions for which to work and with which to do business. More ethical behaviour may make the financial system more stable too, but the recent instability of the financial system had a number of causes. As Christians we should not be surprised by human error or other human imperfections. We need to think carefully about how market structures can minimise the catastrophic effects of human error and also harmoniously combine the beneficial effects of self interest and strongly-held ethical principles.

1 Parts of this chapter are adapted from Chapter One of Booth, *Verdict on the Crash* (2009). Some of the ideas within the chapter have been prompted by the work of other authors in that book.
2 The target is given to the Bank of England by the government and is currently 2%. There is some dispute about the most appropriate measure of inflation. The Bank of England was given a measure that excluded house prices – something that does not appear wise given the role that housing played in the problems that led up to the crash.
3 Indeed, the relatively benign – indeed beneficial – effect that short selling arguably has on financial markets is perhaps indicated by the fact that the Church of England pension fund is happy to facilitate the process through stock lending!
4 See http://www.bankofengland.co.uk/publications/quarterlybulletin/qb070211.pdf
This remark was qualified later in the speech.
5 For example, see a speech by Tony Blair on 8 January 2009: http://tonyblairoffice.org/2009/01/speech-by-tony-blair-at-the-ne.html
6 See the chapters by Anna Schwartz and also by Eamonn Butler in Booth (2009), Woods (2009) and Norgerg (2009).
7 Though, as noted above, it is unlikely that traditional lending would have brought down a UK high street bank – though a Glass-Steagall type Act has not operated in the UK in any case.
8 The extent to which banks finance their activities by borrowing.
9 The excess assets that banks hold to give them a cushion against a fall in the value of their assets.
10 The casual attitude of savers who deposited money in the Icelandic banks that became insolvent is one example of this.
11 A sentiment taken from John Paul II's *Centesimus annus*, but a well known precept in economics. The full quote is: "The social order will be all the more stable, the more it takes this fact into account and does not place in opposition personal interest and the interests of society as a whole, but rather seeks ways to bring them into fruitful harmony."

REFERENCES

Booth P. M. ed. (2009), *Verdict on the Crash,* Hobart Paperback 37, Institute of Economic Affairs, London, UK.
Dembinski P. H. (2009), *Finance: Servant or Deceiver? Financialization at the Crossroads*, Palgrave Macmillan, Basingstoke, UK.
Norgerg J. (2009), *Financial Fiasco*, Cato Institute, Washington DC, USA.
Woods T. E. jr. (2009), *Meltdown*, Regnery, Washington DC, USA.

HOW FINANCIAL INSTITUTIONS DUG THE HOLE WE'RE IN

CATHERINE COWLEY

Following a number of years working in the finance and voluntary sectors, Catherine Cowley entered the Congregation of the Religious of the Assumption. She now teaches ethics, with a particular interest in ethics in the finance sector.

INTRODUCTION

In explaining how financial institutions contributed to the crash there is the danger of presenting it as solely a *technical* failure. Certainly there are many technical factors which contributed: the risk models used; the complexity and opacity of derivatives traded; accountancy rules and so on. At heart, though, the crash was not just a technical failure, it was a *moral* one. A second danger is to view financial institutions as, if not the only culpable parties, then certainly the prime ones with, perhaps, governments and regulators contributing. However, those implicated go far wider than these bodies. In this chapter I shall be explaining how financial institutions got themselves into the situation they found themselves in, but I shall also be describing some of these deeper and wider issues.

SECURITISATION AND MORTGAGE DERIVATIVES

Banks are at the heart of the financial system. Traditionally they have been seen as having two critical functions: the social function of intermediation (that is, facilitating the flow of savings towards investment) and that of risk management. Funds from a myriad of small savers, usually wanting low risk and easy access to their savings, are, through financial intermediaries, used to finance long-term, higher-risk borrowers. Money was lent to companies and to individuals who wanted a loan for a mortgage, car or other high cost item, enabling companies and individuals to smooth 'lumpy' expenditure across time and then the banks collected the repayments of that money for themselves. This way of lending is known as 'originate and hold' because the bank which originated the loan holds on to the loan. In this model the bank has a direct interest in ensuring that the borrower is able to repay.

Starting in the 1970s financial innovation created what is now the dominant model of 'originate and distribute'. Instead of waiting for loans (a typical example being mortgages) to be repaid over many years, lenders began bundling them together into securities representing shares in the previously granted loans (a process known as 'securitisation') and selling them on to other commercial financial institutions. The advantage to the lenders was that they received the money straight away instead of having to wait for the loans to be repaid. They could, therefore, lend more money more quickly to other borrowers. The risk of the loan not being repaid was passed on to those other institutions, which had the advantage of being able to invest in assets that would not otherwise have been available. The risk that the amount of interest received would be less than expected because of a fall in interest rates or early repayment of the loan was also passed on to the institutions that bought the loans. Those risks were reflected in how much institutions were prepared to pay for these 'mortgage backed assets' (MBAs).

Other types of loan were also sold in this way, but for the sake of clarity, and because they were pivotal in the first phase of the crisis, I shall focus on MBAs. MBAs are an example of a derivative. A derivative is a financial contract the value of which is based on (derives from) something else, for example a stock or a barrel of oil or, in this case, loans. These MBAs were arranged in complex ways (known as 'slicing and dicing') to include different amounts of loan principle and layers of interest, and different combinations of risks. Each MBA was given a grade by a rating agency which was meant to reflect how risky it was. AAA is the highest, with gradations down (AA, A, BBB and so on). The higher the rating, the higher the price asked for it.

FINANCIAL HOUSES BUILT ON UNSOUND ASSUMPTIONS

The success of the originate and distribute model rested on a number of key assumptions, all of which needed to be true. These were, first, that risk had been correctly quantified. Crucially, the risk models used for MBAs were based on the belief that the quality of the loans was assured, that house prices would continue to rise as they had in the past and that the level of defaults would remain low. The second assumption was that risk had been correctly rated and, third, that these MBAs were highly profitable. Finally, the fourth assumption was that risk had been dispersed through the financial system because different banks were believed to be exposed, because of this process, to a much wider variety of risks – all of which would not be expected to go wrong at the same time. We now know that all of these assumptions were incorrect.

The quantifying of risk has always been part of a bank's business; the careful assessment of the borrower's ability to repay the loan was vital to the financial health of the lender. The assumption that risk had been correctly quantified seemed reasonable. But the originate and distribute model broke the connection between the lender and the borrower. Instead of a lender having an incentive to be careful to whom it lends and cautious about the amounts of the loan, the incentive became to lend as much as possible and sell on the loan to another institution. There was no direct interest in ensuring that the borrower could repay the loan because, if the borrower defaulted, it was someone else who lost out. Securitisation can be adapted to deal with this problem. For example the purchaser of securities may insist that the originator retains some of the risk, or the rating agencies may look on securities where some risk is not retained by the originator less favourably. However, too little attention was paid to such important details. Instead, looser standards of lending and underwriting of mortgages encouraged reckless lending, particularly to that group known as 'sub-prime' borrowers. These were some of the poorest people with the worst credit histories who could not obtain finance from elsewhere. Usually these mortgages were given with an initial artificially low rate of interest. This not only encouraged people to borrow money they could not afford to repay, it also helped drive up house prices for everyone, confirming – in the short run at least – the belief that house prices would continue to rise. Once interest rates began to rise, defaults in the sub-prime market also rose, the US housing boom ended and prices fell. Defaulting borrowers were unable to sell the asset for enough to repay the loan, as many now had negative equity. The lenders, if they repossessed, were in the same position. Without an assured quality of loan, risk had not correctly quantified.

Risk was also not quantified correctly in another important respect. This was because of the nature of risk in financial markets and what is taken into account when assessing it. Risk is treated as a commodity like any other. Risks can be bought and sold so that every risk has its market and its market price. The most important functions of such a market is to spread the risk and to enable people to carry those risks, and only those risks, that they want to. For example, a person's house will often be a substantial part of that person's total wealth; once it is insured, the risks arising from it catching fire are spread through the insurance market which is happy to absorb that risk from the property owner.

Most trades on the risk markets are not of this kind, however. They are carried out by people who think they have made a better assessment of the risk than others. Stock markets and other security markets function in a similar way to betting on the horses which is simply the aggregate of risks traded by people with different assessments of the outcome of an uncertain event. In horse racing that event might be the winner of the 2.30 at Ascot; in financial markets it is the prospects for a company or, in the case of MBAs, of a default or change in interest rates. In both horse racing and financial markets, the price is determined by people who make different assessments of the same risk. A major difference between these two types of market, however, is that the effects of trading in risk in horse racing are generally confined to market participants. In the type of financial trading discussed here, the effects are, as we have seen, not always confined in the same way.

34

This points to the first flaw in how risk is treated by financial markets. The form of risk-benefit analysis used by financial institutions to evaluate risk considers only the aggregate risks and benefits. What is not considered is the justice of their distribution, that is, who will gain the benefit and who will bear the risks. The evaluation is confined to those who participate in the financial markets and risk is measured in order to safeguard those participants. The question is, is that enough? While it is true that some of the risks are borne by market participants (that is, they may lose profit on a contract), by no means all the risks are borne by them; nor is it true that they bear the most long-lasting consequences. The nature of financial risk in general is such that it may be wholly or largely borne by some people or groups, while the benefits are shared equally, or indeed enjoyed entirely, by different persons from those at risk. Ethically this is always at least questionable. In this financial crash, we have seen that those who enjoyed the main benefits of this trading were not those who have been worst affected by the consequences.

The next problem with risk is that derivatives have become increasingly complex and difficult to evaluate ('opaque' is how they are often described). They were originally created to provide stability and allocate capital to farmers and industry and used for such things as smoothing out cash flows during the year, or hedging against the risk of selling goods abroad. The earliest examples are from Ancient Greece though their main use in this way was from the mid-nineteenth to the mid-twentieth centuries. By the 1990s, however, only about 5% of derivatives were being used in this way; the rest were used for speculation or for other purposes within financial markets. The increase of computer power and the use of complicated algorithms (an algorithm is a step-by-step problem-solving procedure with a precise set of rules) increased their diversity and complexity and also the speed at which they could be traded. By being frequently traded on (often re-sliced and -diced) it was unclear who owned what and with what degree of risk. This uncertainty about the identify of the institution who was actually on the other end of the chain of selling-on (the 'counterparty') and how much risk it was holding was a major factor in the collapse of confidence at the beginning of the credit crunch.

The second assumption of the 'originate and disperse' model was that risk had been correctly rated. As we have seen, however, the amount of risk in these derivatives had not been accurately quantified. This alone would have made the rating given to them by the rating agencies dubious. In addition, however, the conduct of those agencies added to the problem. The data that the agencies used came from the originators of the loans and was taken on trust. As I have already described, the quality of loans had deteriorated and it now appears that some of them were outright frauds: either the borrower could never pay or they were sham loans. Among those arrested (but at the time of writing not convicted) by the US authorities were two former Bear Stearns hedge fund managers. It was the collapse of two Bear Stearns funds and three BNP Paribas hedge funds in July and August 2007 which triggered the credit crunch. These managers are accused of contributing to the collapse of their firm by misleading investors about a fund packed with dubious MBAs. Yet the ratings agencies accepted the data on these, and other, MBAs without checking their sources, whatever they might have suspected about loan quality. They worked on the assumption that the information was accurate.

Determining why they should act in this way would merely be speculation until further investigations are concluded. However, agencies are paid by the institution which needs a rating in order to sell the financial instrument, not by those who wish to buy it. Many large investors, such as pension funds, are only permitted to buy highly rated instruments; so if an instrument is rated as too risky to be considered 'investment grade' the potential market for them shrinks dramatically. If an agency gives too many sub-investment grade ratings, it risks losing future business from the issuing institution, which might go elsewhere for more favourable assessments. Evidence for this belief within agencies is widespread and is generally held to have led to some risky investments being rated as safe.[1] This was despite the history of mortgage-backed securities collapsing in value as they had done in the UK and USA in the 1990s.

The ratings that these assets received is one of the reasons for the third assumption, that is, that they were highly profitable. At one level the reasons why these assets were not as profitable as thought is simply told. As I have already described, much of the data used by the complex computer models was flawed. There were false assumptions about the quality of the underlying loans, that house prices would continue to rise and that default levels would remain at historically low levels. Any one of these factors could have been sufficient to undermine the assets' profitability. Together they were fatal. However, it is necessary to go a little deeper than this if we are to understand what happened and answer the question: if these problems were so fundamental, why were they not spotted and accounted for? We therefore need to look at the behaviour that was generated by the use of these models, as well as by the outcome of profit that they seemed to demonstrate.

To begin with, these models rest on multiple predictions of probability. The positive benefits of the use of probability are enormous. For example, life, health and fire insurance would be impossible without it. Many bridge designs and other engineering feats would never have been evolved. Yet the reliance on probability is fraught with danger. It tends to build on past events and those used prior to the credit crunch were shaped by the amazing stability of key events over many years. The models used for those assets were, in essence, rear-view mirror models. The most obvious problem is that a strategy which worked in the past does not necessarily always work well in the future. Neither do they necessarily incorporate a sufficiently long view to show with any reasonable certainty that a strategy which begins successfully can be carried to a satisfactory completion. A little less obviously, risk models tend to confuse probability with timing: they assume that an event with low probability is therefore not imminent, but low probability events do occur. Some events are simply not amenable to modelling by analytical techniques, such as calculating the probability of human error or illegal activity.

In addition, chaos theory (the effects of the fluttering of the wings of the famous butterfly) should have alerted people to the fact that even very small deviations from multi-levelled probability calculations can have far-reaching consequences. While none of these things in itself is sufficient to negate these types of models, added together they mean that they have a strictly limited usefulness; they are only an educated guess. However, they were too often used as the main – or only- risk measurement and management approach as if they accurately reflected the full reality.

This sort of risk measurement may give an illusory impression of control. Yet derivatives do not eliminate risks; at best they enable that risk to be taken on by those most willing to bear it. There are subtle ways in which attempted control, by creating a false sense of security, compromises our ability to cope. The classic example is the *Titanic*. The new ability to control most kinds of leaks led to the under-stocking of lifeboats, the abandonment of safety drills and disregard of reasonable caution in navigation. Financial institutions, by their reliance on mathematical models, showed the same sort of phenomenon. They assumed that their models gave them control over their risk exposures, leading them to assume far riskier positions that they otherwise would, and to neglect adequate consideration of the extent to which their trading was dependent on leverage – that is to say, borrowing a high percentage of the asking price of the assets they were trading in. More prudential attitudes seemed unnecessary.

This presumption of control was not the only factor pushing the sector into taking on higher levels of risk. One other such factor was bonuses. Many popular commentators have put nearly all the blame for the crash on the 'bonus culture'. They have argued that paying people to take risks would inevitably lead them to take ever greater risks in order to achieve their bonus and that the system fostered outright greed. I have already argued that there were several contributory causes and it would be wrong to suggest that bonuses were the sole culprit. This does not mean, however, that they had no influence. They did, but at a deeper level than that commonly described.

I do not underestimate the motivating power of greed, but it would be wrong to think that this was the only emotion governing behaviour. Another strong emotion at play is the sense of power which many financial practitioners admit they felt. This was the power which comes from knowing that one can buy or sell millions of pounds worth of assets, and that this activity can influence the lives of individuals and companies. It is not a power which is often referred to in the standard explanations of economic behaviour, but it is nevertheless real. Furthermore, it is a power which moves easily into anxiety. Pay, status, even the job itself, are dependent upon meeting ever more stringent performance targets. Extreme competitiveness can be engendered both within an institution (who will get the biggest bonus this year?) and between institutions (outperform Firm X or lose the business of Fund P). Our competitor easily becomes a threat and few of us are at our best when we feel threatened. Illusions of power, anxiety, competitiveness and insecurity are all potent emotions. At the very least they are difficult to bring into harmony with our reason. This is reinforced by the way that jobs and remuneration packages are organised. At one time it was common for bonuses to be paid to a whole team, now they are usually paid to individuals. This change may well weaken a wider sense of the good of the whole institution; now it becomes a much more individualistic concern – particularly where the basis for calculating the bonus is 'you eat what you kill', that is to say, remuneration is calculated according to the amount of fees you generate or profit that you book. In such a situation it becomes even more difficult to maintain a harmony between emotions and reason and for many people it becomes impossible. These emotions affect judgement, the willingness to make perhaps unjustifiably risky investments, to cut corners, to do what has become known as 'gambling for resurrection'.

Such behaviour frequently went unchecked because in a results-dominated culture you do not challenge those who are producing what is demanded. As long as there appeared to be a steady stream of profits few were willing to question the basis or reality of the figures. Even internal procedures made this difficult in a range of institutions. Risk assessment teams have complained that they were often only given a day or so to assess a proposal before appearing before a panel to argue their case against those who have spent weeks or even months developing that proposal. It is not surprising that panels usually accepted the judgement of the developers, backed up, as it appeared to be, by the sophisticated computer models.

This failure to challenge was not limited to managers. Board members were often equally unwilling to go against conventional wisdom. The occasional lone voice raising concerns was easy to dismiss. Institutions, such as a number of Canadian banks, which decided not to follow the strategies being adopted by the majority of their competitors, faced considerable hostility from Boards, institutional investors, analysts and commentators. Their share prices suffered and a number of executives had to struggle to keep their positions, not all successfully. Institutional investors have recently come in for considerable criticism for failing to use their power to question the strategies being aggressively pursued by the majority of banks. However, in one sense it is not surprising that many did not. These institutional investors are often staffed by fund managers who share similar world views, assumptions, pressures from analysts and remuneration packages as those who run the institutions in which they are investing. To challenge the wisdom of the companies in which they hold shares would be to question the very basis of their own position. Thus the behaviour based on the assumption of profitability became widespread and entrenched.

Reality broke in when hedge funds began to collapse in the middle of 2007. The reason that their collapse had such an effect was because the fourth assumption – that risk was dispersed throughout the financial system – was wrong. Market pressures had ensured that an enormous number and range of institutions had traded in these assets. They had been traded on in ever more complex ways so that any initial clarity about the precise constituent elements had been lost. It was almost impossible in many cases to work out who was actually holding which asset, with what level of risk. Because no-one knew who actually held the assets the assumption that risk had been dispersed was always based on faith rather than observable fact. However, the way that the purchase of many of these assets had been financed should also have alerted observers to its falsity. As I have already mentioned, most assets were bought with borrowed funds. This money was frequently borrowed from the very banks who were selling the assets. Thus the risk that the banks thought they had got rid of came back onto their books via the loans that they issued. Furthermore, many banks were also buying this class of assets as a way of boosting their own profits. When the assets fell in value, the institutions that had borrowed money were unable to repay the loans and the banks' own holdings fell in value, leading to losses arriving from two directions at once.

Trying to minimise some of these losses, and compelled by rules about how much capital to hold against certain types of risks, banks tried to sell some of these assets. But they were in a falling market caused by lack of buyers as well as uncertainty about the quality of the assets. Although the ratings agencies were slow to downgrade existing ratings even after the problems within the sub-prime markets had become apparent, when they eventually did so this increased the range of institutions forced to dispose of lower rated assets. This rush of selling forced down prices even further, thereby accelerating the reduction in the value of bank holdings and increasing their losses. Because no-one could now put a price on these assets, and no-one knew who was holding them, banks stopped lending to each other for fear of non-repayment. The inter-bank market froze, liquidity dried up and the credit crunch came upon us.

Financial crises do not respect borders and the effects quickly became global. It became clear that many more banking institutions were at risk from these falling assets, either as lenders or buyers, than had previously been thought. The crisis became worse with a second wave of institutions either failing outright or having to be given government support to survive. This second wave included big mortgage institutions in the US, as well as banks in the UK, US, continental Europe and Iceland amongst others. I shall describe one institution, the insurance company American International Group (AIG) which was rescued, as this illustrates well the point about risk not being dispersed in the way it had been presumed. As the major insurer against credit default, it had become the counterparty to many of the world's largest financial firms. It sat at the heart of a vast network of criss-crossing obligations. If it failed, then that insurance would be lost. In addition, it was a significant borrower in the commercial paper market (that is, bond-like instruments issued by commercial companies) and other public debt markets, and it was a provider of insurance products to tens of millions of customers. If it had collapsed it would have substantially intensified the crisis with hardly a corner of the financial sector untouched. The US authorities decided, therefore, to support it.

ETHICAL QUESTIONS SURROUNDING THE BEHAVIOUR OF BANKS AND BANKERS

In this final section I shall discuss some general ethical questions raised by what happened and I shall begin with the use of derivatives. The present state of affairs sanctions the use of risky derivatives because of the enormous wealth which *may* be created. In general, worries within the financial sector about derivatives seem to centre almost exclusively around the notion that defects may lead to market conditions which would inhibit wealth creation or cause wealth loss. Wealth creation is the only criterion. While it is true that this is an important criterion, it is not true that it should therefore be the only one. Such a position is inadequate. Ethical issues arise in the potential conflict of individual rights and public risks; between my 'right' to invest my money how I will so as potentially to create wealth, and society's interest in maintaining stable economies and protecting the poor. One counter-argument might be based on the claim that wealth is being created, and that is a good. Whilst I accept that wealth creation is indeed a good, I question whether that in fact is what is happening here. Leaving to one side for the moment what has happened over the past two years, I would argue that derivatives frequently do not create wealth. Wealth is certainly re-distributed, but to go back to the comparison with horse racing: if I bet that *Arthur's Ransom* is going to win the 2.30

and you bet that it won't, one of us is going to be wrong. Whoever is right will be wealthier, but the other will be poorer. Wealth has not been created, merely moved around[2]. This is the nature of the type of financial trading that MBAs involve. Indeed, we have seen that wealth is destroyed, but because of the distribution of power among the particular economic agents, those whose wealth has been ruined carried less, or no, weight in the calculations.

Another important question arising from the analysis here concerns the paradoxical nature of our relationship to risk. On the one hand, derivatives help promote a high-risk ethos. On the other hand, their growth points to a deep desire to control and, if possible, eliminate risks. Yet all investments and all loans are risky, because they are based on educated guesses about the future, rather than certain knowledge of what will happen. The search for a risk-free life is a nonsense doomed to failure. Prudence does not mean the avoidance of all risk. An ethic of risk management is required which incorporates both prudence and courage without recklessness because, contrary to popular mythology, managers and financial traders are not paid to take risks, they are paid to know and understand the risks they take.

The issue of bonuses which, for most people, seem staggeringly large, raises a question which goes beyond just the finance sector and involves the whole of contemporary society. It is the question of whether we can still speak of 'enough'. For most onlookers, the response to reports of bonuses in the tens of millions is to say that no-one needs that much, they are just being greedy. But that response is based on a social reality which may no longer exist. To say "I don't need it, I have enough," implies that I have a conception of 'the good life' relative to which terms such as 'need' and 'enough' can be given a determinate meaning and which therefore marks out some things as 'greedy'. Conceptions of the good life have varied hugely, both within and between cultures, but in some sense certain ways of life were seen as intrinsically desirable, that is desirable for itself, not as a means to some further end. Traditionally wealth was thought of merely as a means to the end of the good life; it itself was not an end. Now, for

43

a variety of reasons, the good life is seen, not as something intrinsically desirable, but as that which is desirable simply because it is desired. Desire has no proper end which one can hit or miss, it is something freely chosen and, as long as it does not violate the rights or interests of others, is equal to all others. There is no such thing as *the* good life, only a range of *desirable lifestyles* which are purely individualistic in their selection. What we are left with in the developed world, and increasingly in the developing world, is the conception of the good life put forward by the market. That, however, is precisely based on 'not enough'. There are always more things, more experiences to desire, to aspire towards. Without a socially shared understanding of the good life we have no idea how much money constitutes enough, and therefore where to draw the line and say "that is too much".

And yet for Christians this last issue, along with the others discussed earlier, raises important questions about social justice which cannot be ignored. These are not issues which should just be left to the professionals in the finance sector to sort out, but are ones with which everyone needs to grapple. If the recession has taught us anything, it is that the actions of a numerically small group of people can affect the lives of almost everyone else. We all have a vested interest, therefore, in looking at the root causes and joining in the effort to answer the questions they leave us.

NOTES

1   It could be argued that the regulatory systems that encouraged the purchase of highly rated bonds in various ways were a contributory factor too. However, there is, at the very least, a suspicion that the problems of 'conflicts of interest' that I have described were important.

2   This is not to say that derivatives cannot be used for risk-management and diversification purposes, but a great deal of banks' dealing in derivatives is not for that purpose.

CREDIT, SIN AND
THE 2008 FINANCIAL CRISIS

SAMUEL GREGG

Dr. Samuel Gregg is Research Director at the Acton Institute. He has written and spoken extensively on questions of political economy, economic history, ethics in finance and natural law theory. He is author of the prize-winning The Commercial Society *(2007) and most recently* Wilhelm Röpke's Political Economy (2010).

INTRODUCTION

A predictable by-product of the 2008 financial crisis was a renewed wave of moral condemnation of market capitalism, invariably from those who might be called "the usual suspects". The finance minister of Germany at the time, Peer Steinbrueck, proclaimed, for example, that "Anglo-Saxon" capitalism was finished. Not to be outdone, the Anglican Archbishop of York infamously likened the practice of short-selling to the behaviour of "bank-robbers". Equally unsurprising was the near-universal insistence of leaders of governments, international organisations and many Christian leaders around the world that the key to resolving the financial crisis and preventing similar occurrences in the future was to increase the regulation of banks and the financial industry.[1]

Other commentators have highlighted the extent to which government regulation as well as political manipulation of the US sub-prime mortgage market actually played a major role in facilitating the financial meltdown. Much ink has been spilt detailing the role played by loose and poorly targeted monetary policy – especially by the Greenspan Federal Reserve – in allowing excessive amounts of cheap money to flow into and circulate through the US, and consequently the global economy. Economists of the various neo-classical schools have focused heavily upon the macro-dimensions of the crisis.

If, however, Christians accept that the essence of economic activity, like all human action, consists of individuals and institutions making free choices of a creative and reactive nature, then attention should also be directed to the manner in which credit has been requested and extended by borrowers and lenders throughout the world. In this regard, legitimate questions have been asked about the leverage ratios maintained by major financial houses and banks in the months preceding the crisis. There has, however, been rather more reluctance to analyse and critique the choices made by individual borrowers. This may have something to do with the general climate of moral relativism prevailing in the West, which has infected (and been more-or-less endorsed by) more than one Christian confession, and which discourages people – including some Christians – from critiquing the choices of others in anything other than terms that conform to whatever happens to be politically-correct or fit the *zeitgeist* of the moment.

Thus while various choices made by particular banks, businesses, and financial houses have been heavily – and, in many instances, rightly – criticised on moral and economic grounds, rather fewer moral critiques have been made of the behaviour of individuals who, for example, misrepresented – i.e. lied – about their assets, income, and liabilities in order to obtain loans and mortgages. Base Point Analytics (2007; cf. Mayer, Pence, and Sherlund 2008), for example, found some degree of borrower misrepresentations in as many as 70% of US early payment defaults in a study of three million loans originated between 1997 and 2006. In other words, a good number of mortgage arrangements – many of which were used as the foundation for an increasing number of securities and equities – were based on untruths about assets and untruths about persons. Such actions are already illegal, so extra regulation is unlikely to deter future misrepresentation. Indeed, the only sure way to address this situation is for people to stop lying. Knowing and choosing the truth, it seems, is not as dispensable for harmonious human existence and economic relations as some imagine. A good number of Christians were likely to have been among those misrepresenting themselves, their employment history, and their income, assets and liabilities, as they purchased mortgages. As such, there should be a strong examination of conscience concerning, first, the extent to which they violated orthodox Christianity's absolute prohibition of lying and, second, how their lying may have contributed to the vicious cycle of events that led to the collapse of global financial markets in late 2008.

CAPITAL AND INTEREST

A revealing feature of the analyses of the borrowing and lending habits contributing to aspects of the 2008 financial crisis is that they indirectly underline the extent to which many moral philosophers and economists have forgotten that the extension and seeking of credit was a subject of considerable and often heated discussion for centuries. The very morality of charging interest on loans has been intensely debated by Christian and secular thinkers for over two thousand years. Many contemporary practitioners of finance may be surprised to know that Adam Smith actually favoured usury laws (Smith [1776] 1984, II.iv.14; cf. Paganelli 2008). As John T. Noonan illustrates in his classic study of the Catholic Church's teaching on usury, Christianity's internal debate about this subject led to major clarifications of the nature of money, the development of the first "embryonic theory of economics", and "the first attempt at a science of economics known to the West" (Noonan 1957, p.2).[2] It helped, for example, to establish in theoretical terms when money transcended its character as a means of exchange and assumed the qualities of what we today call "capital".

It may be the case that the relevance of this history for understanding aspects of the 2008 financial crisis and our ability to avoid similar difficulties in the future will become better understood with the passage of time. Of more immediate importance, however, may be growing realisation that if the benefits of borrowing and lending for individuals, institutions and society are to be best realised and extensive regulation avoided, then Christians may need to consider the economic significance – even indispensability – of particular moral habits, or what theologians and philosophers ranging from Aristotle, St Thomas Aquinas, to Adam Smith call 'the virtues'. In the immediate wake of the financial crisis,

Archbishop Vincent Nichols, the Catholic Archbishop of Westminster, was one of the few Christian leaders who underlined this point about the virtues instead of following the uninformed herd and arguing for more extensive regulation of the financial industry.[3]

INDISPENSABLE BASIC VIRTUES

Perhaps the most necessary such habit is the virtue of prudence.[4] The ancient Greeks, the Church Fathers and medieval Christian theologians viewed prudence as the cause and measure of all the non-theological virtues. It expresses the 'perfected ability' of individuals as creatures possessing right reason and free will to make morally-correct practical decisions. A mortgage-lender, for example, draws upon his experience and all the data available to him at a given moment and decides that it is beneficial to extend one person a mortgage while also deciding to deny another person's request for an extension of an existing loan. The mortgage-lender's decisions are the product of an act of prudence (or imprudence), and may involve other virtues such as that of courage (taking a prudential risk on the successful borrower or the risk of upsetting a customer by turning them down) and justice (reflecting carefully upon his decisions because it is what the lender owes in justice to his employer).

Prudence has its own integral parts. Amongst other features, it includes an understanding of first principles (e.g. 'do not steal'); open-mindedness; humility; caution; the willingness to research alternative possibilities; foresight; shrewdness; and the capacity to form an accurate sense of the reality of situations. Without gradually acquiring most or all of these qualities, it is arguable that someone working in the world of finance will either not last very long or will continue to make some very bad decisions. To this extent, prudence allows the practice and institution of credit to play its indispensable role in the modern market economy. Throughout the financial crisis, considerable anger was directed against those who specialise in the credit business, especially sub-prime-lending, be it of mortgages or credit-cards. No doubt, some predatory lending occurred. But why, some argue, should sub-prime-lending businesses exist in the first place? Are they not financial traps for the poor and vulnerable? Do they not discourage prudent saving? There were even calls for official caps on interest-rates offered by private lenders.

The difficulty with some such critiques is that they often reflect fundamental misunderstandings of the nature of credit and its underlying moral apparatus. Credit is about lending others the financial means – the capital – that most of us need at some point of our lives. Whether it is starting a business, taking further education qualifications or buying a house, most people need capital. This means that an entity such as a bank or a private lender has to be willing to take a risk. They do stand to profit if the mortgage is paid off or the business succeeds. But they also lose if a house is foreclosed or a business goes bankrupt. Charging interest is how lenders maintain the value of their loans and make a profit (the margins of which are much narrower than most people realise), thereby increasing the sum-total of capital available in a society. Charging interest is also a lender's way of calibrating risk: the higher the risk, the higher the interest rate in order to compensate for the greater possibility of loss. It follows that if interest-rate ceilings were imposed by government fiat, lenders would effectively be prohibited from charging interest rates commensurate with the risks involved. Hence, lenders would be unlikely to lend capital to entrepreneurs and businesses pursuing high-risk endeavours. Many risky but wealth-creating and employment-generating activities would thus simply never occur. Legislated interest-rate ceilings would also mean that many people of lesser means would never have the chance to acquire the capital they may need, for example, to go to university or start a small business, let alone begin developing a credit-record. Entire categories of people – recent immigrants, the urban poor – could be condemned to life on the margins. Prudence is important in regulating financial relationships but crude government-imposed regulations may well do more harm than good. If prudence does not exist in business relationships it cannot easily be replaced by statutory regulation, which is necessarily indiscriminate.

But at a deeper level, we also forget that while credit is about capital, it is ultimately about something more intangible but nonetheless real. The word "credit" is derived from *credere* – the Latin verb for "to believe" but also "to trust". When Christians recite the *credo*, they are saying not only that they believe in the essential *truth* of the faith, but they are also stating that they trust the witness of the Apostles and others to the life, teachings, death and resurrection of the Lord Jesus Christ. To believe in the Christian Gospel is in part to believe in and place our trust in this witness and on this basis, along with the indispensable workings of God's grace, to take the greatest risk of all, which is the risk of faith in Christ and His Church.

While the analogy is not exact, something similar occurs in the business of credit. Whether it is a matter of giving someone a credit-card for the first time, or extending a business the capital that it needs to grow into a great enterprise, providing people with credit means that you trust and believe in them enough to take a risk on their insight, reliability, honesty, prudence, thrift, courage, enterprise and, above all, their prudence: in short, the moral habits without which wealth-creation cannot occur in the first place, let alone be sustained. A moment's thought about credit should therefore remind us how much the market economy, so often derided by some Christians as materialistic, relies deeply upon a web of moral qualities for its efficacy and sustainability. As the 2008 credit crunch taught us, once these are corrupted – whether by basic dishonesty, excessive regulation, or political manipulation of Fannie Mae and Freddie Mac proportions – the wheels of wealth-creation splutter and eventually grind to a halt; businesses die; people lose their jobs; and families suffer.

MORAL HAZARD AND OCCASIONS OF SIN

When the history of the 2008 financial crisis comes to be written, much attention will undoubtedly be paid to the problem of moral hazard. Moral hazard is a term commonly used to describe those situations when a person or institution is effectively insulated from the possible negative consequences of their choices. This makes them more likely to take risks that they would not otherwise take, most notably with assets and capital entrusted to them by others: the higher the extent of the guarantee, the greater is the risk of moral hazard. Fannie Mae and Freddie Mac are prominent examples of this problem. Implicit in their lending policies was the assumption that, as government-sponsored enterprises with lower capital requirements than private institutions, they could always look to the Federal government for assistance if an unusually high number of their clients defaulted. In a 2007 *Wall Street Journal* article, the Nobel Prize-winning economist Vernon Smith noted that both Fannie Mae and Freddie Mac were always understood as "implicitly taxpayer-backed agencies" (Smith, 2007). Hence they continued what are now recognised as politically-driven lending policies until both suffered the ignominy of being placed in Federal conservatorship in September 2008.

While there is a great deal of literature on the economics of moral hazard, the same material contains curiously little reflection on why the adjective "moral" is attached to the word "hazard". Indeed, when economists started studying the subject of moral hazard in the 1960s, their analysis rarely included an explicitly ethical dimension. For the most part, this remains true today. So why do we not simply describe these situations as instances of "risk hazard"?

It may be that the word "moral" reflects some innate, albeit largely unexpressed, awareness that there is something ethically questionable about creating situations in which people are severely tempted to make imprudent choices. This is, of course, a classic insight derived from the realm of Christian moral theology. The Christian church has always taught that the one who creates "an occasion of sin" bears some indirect responsibility for the choices of the person tempted by this situation to do something very imprudent or just plain wrong. If governments and businesses took moral hazard seriously, they would make an effort to identify those state and non-state structures, policies and practices that create incentives for people to take excessive risks with their own and other persons' assets. They would then do what they could to minimize these instances of moral hazard. The economic benefits would be considerable. Christians could also be more confident that they are doing something to reduce the reach of what might be construed as a structure of sin throughout society.

In a 2007 *Financial Times* column, a prominent member of the former Clinton Administration and now the Obama Administration's economic team, Larry Summers, argued that we should beware of what he called "moral hazard fundamentalism" (Summers, 2007). This was, he said, "as dangerous as moral hazard itself." By this, Summers meant that ruling out extensive government economic intervention on the grounds that it might encourage moral hazard would itself be irresponsible. The problem is that the Keynesian-interventionist outlook associated with widespread government intervention involves, by necessity, a degree of systematic denial of the reality of moral hazard. In an attempt to maintain full employment in perpetuity, Keynesian policies embrace measures ranging from keeping interest-rates artificially low, partially nationalising industries, to engineering large public works programmes. An unfortunate effect is that many businesses as well as ordinary consumers slowly become somewhat insulated from many of the negative consequences of poor decisions and bad investments. As a result, some will become complacent, which is the road to economic stagnation. Others, however, are likely to take risks that become increasingly irresponsible over time until we find ourselves in situations similar to the world economy of 2008.

Of course, Christianity has always proclaimed that human beings are fallible creatures. Many people will take excessive risks at different points in their lives. For some people, it will be with their marriage. Others will behave in an excessively risky manner with their own and others' financial resources. As a consequence, some people will suffer losses. In a society where right reason and the Christian ethic of loving one's neighbour reigns, individuals and communities should be ready to help those in genuine need. Law also has a potentially important role to play. As the legal philosopher John Finnis observes in *Natural Law and Natural Rights* (1980), a sound bankruptcy law can meet all the demands of justice

– legal, commutative and distributive – while respecting the dignity of all those affected, especially the dispossessed, but also those at fault. But Christians do not do anyone any favours by acquiescing in circumstances or incentives that encourage people to behave imprudently and recklessly in the worlds of finance and business.

A RETURN TO PERSONAL RESPONSIBILITY

In the midst of such a financial catastrophe, there is a tremendous temptation for everyone, Christian or otherwise, to blame "the system" or identify groups such as "bankers" as bearing primary responsibility for the financial crisis. Without question, members of some professions, including many in the financial industry, did behave irresponsibly. Those who are Christian ought to be called to account by their Christian community. In this connection, it would also be incumbent upon priests and pastors to ask some very serious questions of the Christians among those politicians who strong-armed government-sponsored enterprises such as Fannie Mae and Freddie Mac into engaging in such irresponsible lending.

But before Christians start engaging in fraternal correction (the old and important Christian tradition of Christians telling their brothers and sisters in Christ where they are failing to live up to the demands of the Christian moral life), we ought to reflect very carefully on our own behaviour and how it may have contributed to the culture of excessive borrowing and lending that underlay much of the 2008 financial crisis. One such question for Christians to ask themselves is to what extent they too have bought into the culture of consumerism.

The problem of consumerism does not arise from the mere fact that every economy has, by definition, producers and consumers. Consumerism is the problem of attaching too much significance to material goods, even to the extent of defining ourselves by the number and type of our possessions, and measuring our worth in terms of what we have compared with others. It is not a problem limited to market economies. Consumerism was equally apparent in Communist command economies, precisely because the absence of material goods meant that people focused enormous amounts of time and their thought upon how to attain and retain more material possessions. Christianity does not, of course, teach that material things are to be despised. Not all Christians are called to a life of asceticism. Indeed, many Christian theologians over the centuries have spoken positively about business, entrepreneurship and the creation of wealth. Christians are, however, called to integrate their ownership and use of possessions into a holistic Christian vision of the purpose and meaning of life revealed to us by Christ. This is as true for those Christians who possess small amounts of wealth as it is for those who possess great wealth.

One practical question for Christians to ask themselves is to what extent they have fallen into consumerist ways of thinking and acting, and how this may have affected their borrowing and lending habits. Obviously there are no hard and fast conclusions to draw here. Everyone's life is different and follows a different path with different challenges and opportunities. There may be occasions, for example, where it is entirely reasonable for a family to borrow money for a vacation, and other occasions when the same family borrowing money for the same purpose is irresponsible. Christians, however, who strive to form their consciences in Christian truth by immersing themselves in the Scriptures and being attentive to the wisdom contained in 2000 years of Christian Tradition will grow immensely in their capacity to discern when they are borrowing responsibly and when their borrowing and spending habits have acquired a consumerist character.

Of course, strongly related to restraining consumption is the importance of saving. Saving to accumulate wealth for its own sake is not to be lauded. Generally, however, the act of saving requires a detachment from immediate gratification which is praiseworthy. Furthermore, saving helps make us less dependent on others as well as providing an independent pool of capital that can allow us to borrow money for various needs in ways that impose less risk on ourselves and others. Once we have provided for our family's basic needs, as well as meeting charitable obligations to others, prudent and moral behaviour does involve making provision for the future by saving and paying down debts. Naturally, the Christian will always bear in mind the folly of building up one's earthly treasures at the expense of our treasure in heaven. But savings may surely also be understood as an act of sound stewardship.

CONCLUSION

In times of crisis, Christians often find themselves in the position of acting yet again as salt and light in the communities in which they exist. This is as true of the 2008 financial crisis and all its consequent effects. Perhaps one of the most significant messages that Christians can impart to the often very secular, even secularist, communities in which they live in the West in the wake of this crisis is that if we want to enjoy the moral and material fruits of economic liberty, then society's moral bonds need to be constantly renewed and strengthened. The alternative is increased regulation, which is often ineffective and counter-productive, not least because of the moral hazard problems invariably associated with regulation. Surely one of the lessons for Christians and non-Christians alike of the 2008 financial crisis is that virtues such as prudence, temperance, thrift, promise-keeping and honesty (not to mention the distinctly Christian emphasis upon not doing to others what we would not want them to do to us) cannot be optional-extras in communities that value economic freedom. If markets are going to work and appropriate limits on government power maintained, then societies require substantial reserves of moral capital. With so many people's economic wellbeing now partly determined by the decisions of those working in financial industries, the virtues (especially that of prudence) should be premium assets sought by banks and financial houses in their employees and directors. Classically understood, virtue ought to be pursued for the sake of human moral flourishing in itself. The Christian knows that the classical virtues of prudence, temperance, courage and justice need to be underpinned, enveloped and completed by the theological virtues of faith, hope and love. But this does not mean that we should close our eyes to the very real economic benefits and stability that may flow from larger numbers of people embracing the virtues, be they theological or classical in nature.

In the end, no amount of regulation – heavy or light – can substitute for the type of moral and character formation that the Christian church once played such an important role in imparting to society. Throughout much of the West, this role has been displaced by aggressive secularist ideologies. Equally damaging has been the efforts of some Christians to reduce the moral demands of the Christian gospel to politically-correct causes and vague appeals to social justice whose content is virtually indistinguishable from the latest left-liberal fad, and invariably reflects that mindset's inherent suspicion of business, finance and the modern market economy. Nature abhors a vacuum. In the wake of the 2008 financial crisis, it may be that Christians have an opportunity to remind Christians and non-Christians alike that there can be no markets without morality.

NOTES

1   This chapter draws upon Gregg (2009) with the kind permission of the publishers, the Institute of Economic Affairs.
2   Perhaps the twentieth-century's foremost modern expert on the subject, Noonan, famously concluded – contra the Archbishop of Canterbury's 2008 assertion that Christianity simply changed its position on money-lending in the sixteenth century – that the Catholic teaching on usury "remains unchanged" (Noonan 1957, p.399). The sin of usury, Noonan states, was always and remains understood as "the act of taking profit on a loan without just title" (Noonan 1957, p.399). Noonan then adds: "What is just title, what is technically to be treated as a loan, are matter of debate, positive law, and changing evaluation. The development on these points is great. But the pure and narrow dogma is the same today as in 1200" (Noonan 1957, p.400).
3   Nichols (2008). This has been re-edited as the introduction to this book.
4   This section draws upon Gregg (2008).

REFERENCES

Base Point Analytics (2007), 'Early Payment Default –
  Links to Fraud and Impact on Mortgage Lenders and
  Investment Banks' http://www.basepointanalytics.com/
  mortgagewhitepapers.shtml

Gregg, Samuel (2008), 'Credit Crunch, Character Crisis',
  Speech delivered to Thomas More Institute and ESCP-EAP
  European School of Management, Wednesday,
  22 October.

Gregg, Samuel (2009), 'Moral failure: Borrowing, Lending,
  and the Financial Crisis', in Philip Booth (ed.), *Verdict on
  the Crash: Causes and Policy Implications*, London: IEA,
  pp.145-156.

Mayer, Christopher J., Karen M. Pence, and Shane M.
  Sherlund (2008), *The Rise in Mortgage Defaults*,
  Washington, D.C.: Finance and Economics Discussion
  Series, Divisions of Research & Statistics and Monetary
  Affairs, http://www.federalreserve.gov/Pubs/feds/2008/
  200859/200859pap.pdf

Nichols, Vincent (2008), "Homily at Civic Mass, Sunday,
  23 November 2008".

Noonan, John T. (1957), *The Scholastic Analysis of Usury*,
  Harvard, MA: Harvard University Press.

Paganelli, Maria Pia (2008), "*In Medio Stat Virtus*: An
  Alternative View of Usury in Adam Smith's Thinking",
  in Sandra J. Pearl and David M. Levy (eds.) *The Street
  Porter and the Philosopher*, Ann Arbor, MI: University of
  Michigan Press, pp.202-227.

Smith, Adam [1776] (1984), *An Inquiry into the Nature
  and Causes of the Wealth of Nations*, R.H. Campbell,
  A.S. Skinner, and W.B. Todd (eds.), Indianapolis, Liberty
  Classics.

Smith, Vernon L. (2007), "The Clinton Housing Bubble",
  Wall Street Journal, 18 December.

Summers, Lawrence (2007), "Beware Moral Hazard
  Fundamentalism", *Financial Times*, 23 September.

ETHICAL PERSPECTIVES ON THE BEHAVIOUR OF BANKS

IAIN ALLAN

Professor Iain Allan is a Visiting Professor at Cass Business School, London, UK. During forty years in financial businesses, Iain worked for mutual life insurance companies, a stockbroking partnership and two large international banks. Iain is an actuary, from Edinburgh in Scotland. He became an elder of the Church of Scotland in 1974.

―――――

INTRODUCTION: RULES V ETHICS

Ahead of and during the financial crisis, dealers in many large international banks observed internal and regulatory risk controls, but built up concentrated exposures in what turned out to be very risky assets. The management of these banks gave accurate views of their positions, to the best of their knowledge at the time, but often came back soon afterwards to report greater losses and the need to raise additional capital. At the same time, bank regulators met their obligations of supervision and control but, like others, failed to anticipate the extent of the problems across the banking system and then found it difficult to deal quickly with problems as they arose. How was it that everybody followed their well-established rules, but a situation developed which seemed to threaten the global banking system and even the free-market economy worldwide?

As the financial crisis moved from the front page to the inside pages, another story hit the headlines in the UK – MPs' expenses. In the UK, MPs are allowed to claim expenses for the cost of running a second home. However, a leading newspaper, the *Daily Telegraph*, revealed that some MPs in each of the main parties seemed to be abusing the system, claiming for such items as cleaning a moat and building a floating house for ducks on a pond, claiming interest on mortgages which had been repaid and changing the designations of second homes to avoid capital gains tax. Many of the named MPs attempted to justify their behaviour by claiming that their expense claims were within the rules and had been approved by the appropriate body, but public opinion was strongly of the view that many of the claims were extravagant and unreasonable.

The issue of MPs' expenses shows that public opinion had a clear and quite uniform view of what was fair and reasonable, and what was not, regardless of what could be justified under the rules. Was there a parallel in the financial crisis? While participants followed the rules, did the behaviour of some or all of them fall short of the ethical standards that society would expect, and did this to some extent cause, or exacerbate, the financial crisis?

ETHICS

One ethical approach is to be a good citizen by complying with rules and regulations. But, as Audi (2009) said: "Ethics requires more of us than does any reasonable body of laws" (page 21). When we talk as Christians about ethics, we generally mean "virtue-based" ethics, which were put forward by Aristotle and developed by Thomas Aquinas and others.

Jacobs (2005) commented on Aristotle (364-22 BC): "His 'Nicomachean Ethics' is a foundational work in virtue-based theorising... Aristotle held that there are intellectual virtues and virtues of character, the latter acquired through habituation... Another key part of his view is that ethics cannot be codified, nor is there some single fundamental principle or criterion of right action... There are certain virtues the excellent person must have, and there are certain ethical rules the agent acts on, but ethics overall is a matter of judgement that is carefully calibrated to the features of particular situations. It is not simply or mainly a matter of rule-following" (pages 15-16).

Of Thomas Aquinas (1225-74), Jacobs (2005) said: "...there are substantial affinities between Aristotle and Aquinas, and Aquinas certainly regarded Aristotle's thoughts as a pinnacle of rational understanding, though incomplete on account of not knowing of the Christian revelation. Because of the depth of his understanding of Aristotle and because of the richness of his own thought, Aquinas's works are attracting growing contemporary interest. It is increasingly recognised that it is not correct to regard Aquinas simply as 'Aristotle plus Christianity'. The interest in his ethical thought tends to be focused on its value to current developments and defences of virtue-centred moral psychology and moral theory" (page 14).

Personal ethics

Most of us will have a similar experience of being taught rule-based ethics and then learning virtue-based ethics. Brought up in a coal-mining town near Edinburgh, in Scotland, I was encouraged by my parents to follow a simple set of rules such as telling the truth, not stealing, getting on with my two brothers and being polite to older people. Looking back, there were rules for my own behaviour, for my behaviour in the family and for my behaviour in relation to other people. Sadly, my behaviour did not always live up to the rules, and sometimes it took courage to follow the rules.

As I grew older, behavioural principles were established at home from the example of my parents, including their generous contribution to community activities. Also at home, daily discussions over the family dinner table showed that there could be different points of view about moral issues, and that the appropriate ethical behaviour might depend on the circumstances[1]. The development of virtue-based ethics was re-enforced at the Presbyterian Church of Scotland, where the format was relatively austere and the minister's sermons, the high point of the weekly services, gave simple, clear messages about the need to show consideration for other people and Christian compassion to those in less fortunate circumstances as well as about the need to believe in God.

Business ethics

I started work in 1969 at a mutual[2] life insurance company in Edinburgh, training as an actuary, and then, after qualifying, moved to a stockbroking partnership in London. Somewhat surprisingly, I found the values and behaviours in both businesses, while not overtly religious, very similar to those I had experienced at home and school and at church. In both of them, the senior management and partners encouraged good behaviour, hard work and career progression, and set high standards by their own examples. In both cases, there were good friendships and social activities with work colleagues. Both organisations were free from the short-term pressures of reporting to shareholders and could take a long-term view in doing what they believed to be right. In both companies, good behaviour was reinforced by the threat that, as a result of bad behaviour, membership of the professional body could be removed, making future employment in the same field impossible.

I subsequently worked for two large international banks, and found their corporate culture and behaviour to be similar in many ways to those I had previously experienced, but different in others. Similarities included the qualities of trust and integrity, which are obviously necessary for confidence in banks. The senior executives worked hard and were very committed, although they were not very visible to the large and dispersed staff. Teamwork was encouraged and there were sporting and social activities. Collectively, senior management aspired to treat customers and employees well, and better than the minimum required by law. Of course, this could simply have reflected good business sense, to generate sustainable profits for shareholders, rather than fundamental ethical consideration. Share ownership and bonuses were powerful incentives to perform well, but they could also encourage self interest and a focus on short-term performance. Differences between the two international banks and the mutual and partnership organisations of my earlier career included a strong focus on rules and regulations, with the danger that this could crowd out considerations of appropriate ethical behaviour.

Banks strongly rules-based

External and internal requirements cause banks to be strongly rules-based organisations. In the first place, banking is a regulated industry and regulators such as the Securities and Exchange Commission (SEC), in the United States, and the Financial Services Authority (FSA), in the United Kingdom, impose many rules. Also banks, like other companies, must observe accounting rules and standards when publishing their results and making other disclosures. As it happens, in the period ahead of the financial crisis, complicated new rules were introduced for capital adequacy and fair value accounting, and the need for many experienced risk and accounting employees to focus on the implementation of the new regulations may have distracted their attention from spotting the deteriorating economic trends.

In addition to having to observe external regulations, banks tend to be very large organisations and, like other large organisations, operate through fairly rigid structures, with their own rules for employees at all levels. Also banks, possibly like other large companies, may have dedicated departments for corporate and social responsibility, and this can encourage employees to leave it to the corporate and social responsibility specialists to focus on ethical issues and to produce rules for them to follow.

Junior employees

Account opening procedures are heavily regulated, to avoid money laundering. In a local branch, an employee may think it ethical to open an account for a customer whom he or she has known for many years without proof of identity by passport or utility bills, but this could lead to the bank being fined by its regulator. In the past, banks failing to comply with account opening, or similar, procedures have been fined one or two million dollars by their regulator.

Giving advice to customers is strictly controlled by compliance regulations, to avoid mis-selling. An employee may have a view about which product would be right for a customer, but must collect detailed information about the customer's financial position and follow rules which guide the employee to the most appropriate product to meet the needs of the customer.

Middle managers

A principal risk in commercial banking is the possibility of bad debts on loans to customers. For most loans to personal customers and to small and medium-sized companies, lending decisions have been centralised and in some cases automated. Experience has shown that, if lending officers are given discretion on lending, they are likely to be too keen to support their customers and do business, and so may increase risk to the bank. So their discretion is very limited and they have to follow the rules.

A regrettable aspect of banks – and, possibly, of other large companies – is that middle managers, looking for progress and promotion, may find it safer to just follow the rules than to consider and do what seems right and is within the rules. They may believe that they would gain little from applying their discretion based on ethical (or other) considerations if the decision turned out well but would have much to lose from using their discretion if the decision turned out badly. Middle management therefore becomes used to following the rules and does not develop the discretion or ethical compass that may be necessary higher up the organisation.

Senior management

Senior management must establish frameworks to ensure that regulations relating to many areas such as account opening, risk management, capital adequacy and financial reporting are being observed and that all necessary reports are being submitted. Banks support a broad range of corporate customers, which may be active in areas such as tobacco, alcohol, arms, oil pipelines or nuclear power stations, which may be considered either not ethical or not 'environmentally friendly'. However, if banks were to refuse to support businesses in these areas, even if they are legal and comply with environmental standards, they could damage employment prospects in communities where they operate and could cause criticism from the media that it is not right for banks to make moral judgements on behalf of their customers. It is therefore understandable that banks may take the view that they should be willing to do business which is legal and which meets their financial objectives, although some banks will choose not to do so.

It can be difficult for the senior management to agree ethics-based decisions, even when they want to. Large banks employ people from many businesses and from many countries: their different experience and backgrounds bring many strengths, but there may not be a homogeneous culture or a shared understanding of ethical issues. As an extreme example, a payment that might be regarded as an incentive payment in some countries might be seen as a bribe in others. It would therefore not be surprising if banks developed a culture whereby they were willing to undertake any activity that is legal.

POTENTIAL LIMITATION OF A STRONGLY RULES-BASED CULTURE

An important potential limitation of a strongly rules-based culture is that, although information may be well disseminated downwards through a systematic process, information other than that required under reporting rules may not always pass freely up the organisation. Junior employees may feel that it is not their responsibility to raise issues. Even when they do, middle managers are not necessarily good at passing on information relating to problems or potential problems, and may be afraid of "rocking the boat". And senior managers, despite good intentions, never have as much time as they would like to visit people in their operating businesses – partly, in the UK, ahead of the recent financial crisis, because senior management had to spend a lot of time focusing on new regulations and on competition enquiries.

However, it is also possible that, in the management of banks ahead of the crisis, there was a degree of complacency, or even hubris, because there had not been a major recession worldwide since the oil crises of the 1970s. There were signs of booms in the rising prices of commodities and of shares in emerging markets, in the size and leverage of private equity transactions and, of course, in the strong growth in house prices and mortgage lending in many countries. Surely front-line dealers must have recognised that the rising trends in these markets could not go on for ever, and could be followed by busts, but they may have been influenced by the emotions which have occurred before in such booms – greed to participate in rising markets and fear of missing part of the rise by selling too soon – as well as by their incentive structures, which promised large bonuses in good times but did not threaten negative bonuses in bad times. Whether front-line dealers experienced such sentiments or not, and whether or not they attempted to inform their managers of possible risks, and whether or not senior management was interested in cautionary voices, the boards of the affected banks did not seem to fully recognise the severity of the situation until it was effectively too late for them to take defensive actions.

An article in a UK newspaper, *The Sunday Times*[3], about Larry McDonald, a former Lehman Brothers trader, suggested that there had been a "divide between the boss and employees", and said of the apparent breakdown in communications at Lehmans: "In the four years McDonald worked for the company he never once saw Fuld. His superiors never saw Fuld either. This lack of interaction meant that warning calls from the frontline were not heard, and certainly not heeded, in the years leading to the collapse".

The toxic securities

At the heart of the financial crisis were complex securities known as collateralised debt obligations (CDOs). Although banks' activities relating to CDOs were unquestionably legal, and were approved by boards and regulators, they did raise some important and fundamental ethical questions. Banks with a strongly rules-based culture were perhaps not well equipped to deal with these ethical questions.

Business model

In the US, it had become normal practice for local brokers to "originate" mortgages (that is, to lend money to personal customers against the security of their homes), and then to sell packages of mortgages to banks which would convert them into securities known as mortgage-backed securities (MBSs) and "distribute" these securities (that is, sell them to a range of investors, mainly institutional investors). This "originate and distribute" business model was consistent with the fundamental role of banks as intermediaries between savers and borrowers. In the years ahead of the financial crisis, US interest rates were low, to encourage economic recovery after the setback which was caused by the dotcom fall-out and by the mood of caution which prevailed after 9/11. Reflecting the low interest rates, and the limited risk in mortgages while house prices were rising, yields on standard mortgages were also low and investors became more willing to invest some of their funds in sub-prime mortgages because of their higher yields, despite their higher risks.

To offer securities with higher yields than on standard mortgages, but with risk reduced by diversification, banks created CDOs that contained a mixture of MBSs including sub-prime elements. Because of the perception that the diversification would reduce risk, many of these CDOs were rated AAA by the credit rating agencies (that is, the top grade, which would be applied to strong governments and companies), although they offered yields above other AAA bonds to an extent that would normally have indicated a significant degree of risk. Financial lead had been turned into financial gold. Ethical questions relating to banks' activities in sub-prime mortgages and in MBSs based on them include whether the AAA rating of CDOs should have been believed, given the higher risk of sub-prime mortgages, whether the business model extension from standard mortgages to sub-prime mortgages was consciously approved, or just happened, whether front-line specialists simply followed the rules in reporting their positions, or recognised their ethical responsibility to make their managers aware of the risk characteristics of CDOs and other similarly complex securities, and whether managers adequately explained the nature of CDOs and their risks to senior management and to board members.

Origination

In the US, as in many other countries, house prices increased strongly and the volume of mortgages grew rapidly in the years ahead of the financial crisis, and the securitisation business boomed. So some investment banks such as Lehman Brothers and Merrill Lynch bought mortgage origination brokers to secure their supply of mortgages for securitisation and distribution. In the regional businesses acquired, it was much more difficult to control compliance than in centralised institutional businesses and there was some misrepresentation of customer information to obtain mortgages and a focus on generating sub-prime mortgages. The first of these behaviours is clearly unethical; the second raises a fundamental question as to whether it is ethical for banks to provide mortgages to customers who may not be able to maintain their payments and who, in the event of default, are likely to experience serious financial and mental pressures. This question is particularly important in the United States, where legislation bans the selective avoidance of lending to less affluent groups and so contributed to a central cause of the crisis. Regulation, in effect, encouraged or required a practice that some would consider unethical or uneconomic or both.

Distribution

At the other end of the business model, another ethical question relates to the distribution of these CDO securities to investors. Clearly, large institutional investors are expected to look after themselves and to make their own decisions about which securities to buy and to sell, but a broad range of investors could not possibly have had the resources to analyse the complex CDOs, and must have relied on the ratings given by the credit rating agencies, supported by the reputations of the issuing banks.

Rating

MBSs and CDOs were individually rated by credit rating agencies, such as Standard & Poor's and Moody's, who received fees for analysing them and rating them. The AAA ratings given by credit rating agencies to many MBSs and CDOs gave comfort to banks' management and to regulators, as well as to investors. To an external observer, it now seems incredible that CDOs containing some exposure to sub-prime mortgages, however diversified, could have been rated AAA, given the very substantial losses that have occurred. Were the credit rating agencies influenced by self-interest in generating fee income, were the models used by the credit rating agencies faulty, or did investors just not understand the meanings of the credit ratings? In relation to fee income, Soros (2009) commented: "The process was driven by the pursuit of fee income... Moody's revenues from structured products were on par with revenues from its traditional bond rating business" (page 86). In relation to the models, Soros (2009) said: "Since the rating agencies based their valuations on past loss experience, and loss experience improved during rising house prices, the rating agencies became increasingly generous in the valuations of collateralized mortgage obligations" (page 85).

To the extent that the credit ratings were based on past trends, including rising house prices, they were clearly of limited value when house prices started to go down. Morrison (2009) commented: "Ratings are supposed to tell us the likelihood that a bond will make the repayments it promised on time, and in full. The precise interpretation of this state-ment varies from one agency to another. ...Notwithstanding minor differences of definition, all of the ratings have one feature in common: they fail to distinguish between defaults that occur during economic booms, and those that occur during downturns... Rating agencies do not pretend to account for the cyclicality of default, so, arguably, investors are at fault when they fail to adequately account for it when selecting investments" (pages 120-121). To make matters worse, as US house prices fell and the financial crisis developed, credit rating agencies downgraded their ratings of CDOs, depressing their prices further not only because of their lower rating but also because of forced selling by investors not allowed to hold securities with ratings lower than AAA.

Retention

The banks' business model had been to buy packages of mortgages from originators, securitise them and distribute the securities to investors. As the crisis developed, banks retained substantial positions in CDOs on their trading books, either because they chose to retain some exposure to show their own confidence in the CDOs they were selling to investors, or because they found it increasingly difficult to sell them to investors as the crisis developed, or because their dealers in these securities chose to hold or even buy them, when they were rated AAA, to take advantage of their yields that were higher than those available on other AAA securities.

One of the key issues in the financial crisis is the suspicion that the dealers of the banks that accumulated substantial positions in CDOs with sub-prime exposures were influenced by the expected positive impact on their own bonuses. Bank dealers generally receive a percentage of the income that they generate, and so expected that the high yields on the CDOs which they held for the bank would increase their bonuses, even though bonuses paid to dealers already seemed unimaginably large to most people.

Valuation

As US house prices declined and the financial crisis deepened, problems relating to the valuation of CDOs began to become visible. Under accounting rules, had the banks owned the underlying mortgages, or other loans, losses would have been taken in the banks' accounts as they arose. In past periods of economic difficulties, losses occurred over a period of years and banks could widen their margins to offset the loan losses to some extent. However, on this occasion, the mortgages had been converted into securities and had to be valued at fair value – either market value, or an estimate of it. As the situation deteriorated, the values of CDOs fell sharply because they reflected at once the more negative outlook and the expected losses on the underlying mortgages in future years, even before these losses actually occurred.

However, because there were very few transactions in these securities, the amount of losses had to be determined by valuations based on complex technical models. Confidence in the models had already been eroded by their failure to anticipate the extent of the risks. Investors did not feel comfortable with values derived from the models, and were concerned that they might be higher than fair values should be. On the other hand, values based on such transactions as were reported seemed lower than fair values should be, because of forced selling. So, despite the growing evidence of very large losses across the banking system, it was difficult to establish the total amount of losses or their distribution across banks, and the resulting prolonged uncertainty was very damaging for confidence in banks.

Collateralised debt obligations

By investing in CDOs, it was possible to suffer large losses in adverse circumstances – which may have been thought unlikely, but did actually happen. On CDOs, assessments of risk, and valuations, had to be based on models of such complexity that it was unlikely that board and management personnel, except those responsible for the banks' activities in CDOs, would have the technical skills to understand the models and their limitations and shortcomings. So was it ethical for banks to develop CDOs and distribute them to their customers?

Furthermore, was it ethical for banks to invest their shareholders' funds in CDOs? Commercial banks are heavily regulated and shareholders in them are entitled to regard them as safe long-term investments, although with some cyclicality reflecting higher bad debts and lower profits in times of economic weakness and vice versa. Investors in commercial banks expect to benefit from the value created from long-term relationships with personal, business and corporate customers. Investors should understand that there may be some trading activities to support customer-facing activities, but would expect the risks of such trading to be strictly controlled, especially in relation to risky securities such as CDOs. Investors in investment banks should expect more "proprietary" trading (that is, trading for the banks' own accounts), but not to such an extent that it might put the bank at risk. Distinction should be made between, on the one hand, the legitimate, and ethical, banking business of providing borrowers with mortgages and investors with securities based on them, and the limited trading which may be necessary to support these activities, and, on the other hand, using shareholders' capital to speculate in risky securities such as CDOs – an activity which may have been in the mind of Lord Turner, Chairman of the FSA, when he talked about banks' "socially useless activities".[4] It is not *de facto* unethical for banks to engage in such trading. The shareholders in some banks, especially investment banks, may wish to be exposed to such risks. However, directors and senior managers should not use the assets in a way that shareholders would not expect them to be used.

FINANCIAL REPORTING

Commentators on the financial crisis have asked if it could be right that some banks which had, in the autumn of 2007, disclosed exposures to US sub-prime mortgages, sounded quite positive in the first quarter of 2008 when reporting their results for 2007, but came back soon afterwards to disclose significantly higher losses and the need to raise additional capital from existing shareholders, sovereign wealth funds or from governments.

When the banks announced their 2007 results, these results had of course been scrutinised and approved by their auditors. A point of particular concern was the valuation of CDOs by models or by reference to such limited transactions as were made. But the values estimated and published were approved by the auditors as representing fair value at the time of the accounts. While the reported results were legally correct, there were at the time widespread concerns that US house prices, and the values of mortgage-related securities, would decline further. Banks were no more able than anyone else to predict the future, or to anticipate that US investment bank Lehman Brothers would be allowed to fail in September after the broadly similar investment bank Bear Sterns had been rescued in April. However, in the then prevailing climate of anxiety about banks, an apparently more ethical approach might have been to present a sober view of the situation and prospects, and possibly to comment on mistakes which had been made, lessons learned and actions taken or planned.

However, it is not certain that shareholders would have responded well to such honesty. In business as in politics, there seems to be an expectation of "spin", with upbeat, positive messages. So, in particular, if banks had tried to be helpful by indicating their potential losses from a range of scenarios which were by then clearly possible even if they were still considered unlikely, their share prices might have fallen sharply and accelerated the crisis which subsequently happened, with no benefit to any of the stakeholder groups.

SHAREHOLDERS

At times during the crisis, selling by shareholders and short-selling by hedge funds (selling shares they did not own in the hope of buying them back cheaper, later) led to sharp falls in the share prices of many banks. A perception that hedge funds were behaving in an inappropriate manner was apparently justified when a temporary ban on the short selling of many financial shares was introduced in the autumn of 2008. But was the behaviour of shareholders and hedge funds unethical? Selling by shareholders and short-selling by hedge funds were particularly evident in two periods. Towards the end of 2007, concerns were growing about potential losses from sub-prime exposures across the banking system, without clear information about where the exposures and the risks lay. Falling share prices forced disclosures by banks about the extent of their sub-prime exposures. Later, in the autumn of 2008, further sharp declines in banks' share prices, to very low levels, forced measures to resolve the uncertainties of a number of large banks in the United States and in Europe, by one means or another.

Selling by shareholders was legal, as was short-selling by hedge funds, except during the temporary ban. There is a strong case for asserting that selling and short-selling were also ethical and that, although they caused unwelcome pressure at the time, action was required, and the sharp falls in banks' share prices created a sense of urgency and forced quicker and greater responses than might otherwise have happened. In addition to capital injections into banks and guarantees for some risky loans, these responses included rapid reductions in interest rates to almost zero in the US and in the UK, the injection of further funds through a process known as quantitative easing, and fiscal expansion packages in many countries. Without the selling and short-selling of bank shares, and the strong policy responses, the recession might well have been deeper and longer.

CONCLUSION: RULES AND ETHICS

To avoid a recurrence of the recent banking crisis, various reforms to banks have been proposed. It has been suggested that banks should hold more capital, that non-executive directors should have banking experience or training, that shareholders should be more engaged and that there should be controls on the size and form of bonus payments. However sensible and well meaning, it is doubtful if regulations to implement such suggestions would have averted the recent financial crisis. No amount of capital that was reasonable for normal circumstances would have been enough to cope with the substantial losses reported by some banks. Banking experience would not normally include detailed technical understanding of CDOs and the ability to assess the risks inherent in them. In both Bear Sterns and Lehman Brothers, employees were large shareholders, should have understood the issues and should have been able to bring pressure on the management, but they did not prevent their failure. Schemes could be devised to circumvent controls on bonuses: for example if bonuses had to be deferred, employees could take out loans against deferred bonus payments.

More fundamentally, compliance with the rules did not prevent the recent financial crisis, and the imposition of yet more rules might only exacerbate the existing tendencies to rely on the rules rather than to consider the appropriate ethical behaviour to control risks and to believe that increased regulation can prevent the recurrence of the recent financial crisis.[5]

Looking to the future, there are likely to be more booms and busts. Learning from the recent financial crisis, there is a case for banks adopting what might be called an ethics-based approach and also openly debating and deciding what is right in the particular circumstances. They should act with greater humility and less hubris, recognising that there may be problems within the business and trying to identify them at an early stage when it might still be possible to do something about them. At such an early stage, a sense of impending dangers may not be evident in the figures reported to management, but might be in the minds of front-line staff. Access to such insight could be achieved in two ways. Firstly, the directors could be more engaged with the businesses, without undermining the authority of the chief executive, and so sense potential problems at an early stage. Secondly, and probably more importantly, employees should feel able to raise concerns at an early stage, even though they may not have evidence to support their concerns, without fears that there would be a "shoot the messenger" response, or that they might even be forced to leave for what might be perceived as disloyal criticism of colleagues and superiors.

In this context, it was encouraging to hear, on a UK radio programme[6] on RBS, the following comments by Andrew Kirkby, of RBS Investment Banking, on his new chief executive: "Stephen is making it very clear that he wants people to be accountable, to raise issues, and I think that he is certainly a proponent of a culture where if people feel there is an issue to be addressed by senior management they shouldn't be frightened to put up their hand, and part of that is people feeling that they're not going to be punished if they do actually identify issues they feel need to be addressed."

Given the adverse publicity surrounding banks and the apparent greed of their dealers, Christians may think that they should not work in banks. The reverse is the case. Banks provide important financial services that make our lives easier. They support economic growth. They are among the largest employers, and offer a broad range of careers. Our pension funds have investments in them. We all benefit from their success. Christians with appropriate skills and experience should want to work in banks in all areas and at all levels, and in doing their own jobs with a strong commitment to ethical behaviour, exert a positive influence on their culture and behaviour. It may seem difficult to change the established culture of a large organisation. However, the recent financial crisis has illustrated the need for a new and better approach, and the topic of MPs' expenses showed that most people have a mature and shared view of what is right and what is wrong. Against this background, the contribution of Christians could have a positive, catalytic effect on banks doing what is right, as well as what is consistent with the rules.

NOTES

1   Moral values, of course, are not a matter of opinion to a Christian. However, the precise form of more detailed ethical codes and behaviour may differ, depending on the circumstances. For example, hard work may be regarded as morally virtuous, but it would not be ethical to work so hard that one neglected the needs of one's family.

2   A mutual life insurance company is owned by its policyholders, rather than by shareholders.

3   *The Sunday Times* Business Section, 30 August 2009.

4   Round-table discussion organised by current affairs magazine *Prospect*.

5   It is also worth mentioning that this is not just an issue of ethical behaviour. Directors and senior management need to have an intuitive understanding of the risks the business is taking that goes beyond that provided by quantitative models. Again, more rules and regulations may impede management and directors from obtaining such an intuitive understanding and communicating its importance to junior managers.

6   BBC Radio 4 programme Rebooting RBS, 26 August 2009.

REFERENCES

Audi R. (2009), *Business Ethics and Ethical Business*, Oxford University Press, Oxford, UK.

Calverley J.P. (2009), *When Bubbles Burst*, Nicholas Brealey Publishing, London, UK.

Collins J. (2009), *How The Mighty Fell*, Random House Business Books, London, UK.

Dow C. (1998), *Major Recessions*, Oxford University Press, Oxford, UK.

Jacobs J.A. (2005), *Ethics A-Z*, Edinburgh University Press, Edinburgh, UK.

Mason P. (2009), *Meltdown*, Verso, London, UK.

Morrison A.D. (2009), contributor to *Verdict on the Crash*, edited by Booth P.M., Hobart Paperback 37, The Institute of Economic Affairs, London, UK.

Muolo P. And Padilla M. (2008), *Chain of Blame*, John Wiley & Sons, Hoboken, New Jersey, US.

Painter-Morland M. (2008), *Business Ethics as Practice*, Cambridge University Press, Cambridge, UK.

Edited by Singer P. (2008), *A Companion to Ethics*, Blackwell Publishing, Oxford, UK.

Soros G. (2009), *The Crash of 2008 and What it Means*, PublicAffairs, New York, US.

Steare R. (2009), *Ethicability*, Roger Steare Consulting Limited, London, UK.

USURY AND BAILOUTS – MORALLY DOUBTFUL AND MORALLY DISASTROUS

ANDREW LILICO
Chief Economist, Policy Exchange

———

In this chapter, I wish to consider two key connected moral issues that have arisen in the context of the credit crunch:

- The morality of usury.
- The morality of bailouts in general, and the bailouts of 2008 in particular.

The connection between them should become clear.

USURY

By "usury" I shall initially mean simply the practice of lending money at interest – it is thus to be distinguished from, for example, taking an equity stake in a business.

As a modern economist, I have tended to think about borrowing as simply an allocation of my saving decisions in time. I could save before I purchase a particular good by saving, perhaps in a bank, and earning interest as a result of the bank lending the money to someone else. Alternatively, I could save up after I make the purchase by initially taking out a loan, then make the purchase and save to pay back the loan later. Being able to decide, according to my own convenience, in which periods of my life I spend more than I earn and in which I earn more than I spend (and therefore save) enables me to smooth consumption across my lifetime, increasing my utility. It allows me, for example, to retire in old age on my savings and buy some basic consumer goods if I am a poor college student with good earnings potential. The interest I receive in periods during which I save reflects the riskiness of the assets in which I save, whilst the interest I pay in periods in which I borrow reflects the riskiness I present to my creditors.

Now this story is all very well, and indeed there is one really key element in it: the notion that money put in a bank is money lent to someone – it is an investment. But the credit crunch and its aftermath have placed in sharp relief our society's extensive use of debt. Certain specific forms of borrowing were intimately involved in the credit crunch itself, and with the UK and US now exposed as amongst the most privately indebted countries of all time, it is of interest to reflect upon the morality of lending in general, and not just in the specific technical forms most central to the progress of the credit crunch.

I note that there are many issues associated with the morality of borrowing, the indulgence of greed and impatience, and the virtues of self-restraint, abstinence and delayed gratification. These issues are important and highly relevant, but I shall not, in the main, be discussing them here.

A brief timeline of the debate about usury

From the period of classical Greece until the seventeenth century, there was an extremely active debate concerning the morality of usury. Without becoming bogged down in historical detail that is not central to our considerations here, one might roughly characterise this debate as follows:

- First, following the development of money and then monetary lending, certain practical problems arose with lending at interest.

- Next theorists such as Aristotle, Cato and Seneca addressed the question of what might be the theoretical problems underlying these practical difficulties. By Roman times lending at interest had a very bad moral reputation.

- Early Christianity (and thence Islam) took on board the cultural Roman assumptions concerning the immorality of usury, indeed in some areas becoming stricter, and only gradually, by the Middle Ages, developed the view that there was no strong scriptural basis for opposing usury outright, and that instead, although usury presented moral challenges, there were circumstances in which it could be justified. Central to these were the concepts of compensation for default costs and for the risk of loss. (Aquinas and his followers had, however, developed further Aristotle's original conceptual objection, arguing that money is consumed in its use, like food and unlike, say, a table.)

- At around the time of the Reformation, Catholic thought, as represented by Eck, for instance, was seeking to liberalise further, permitting much higher rates of interest under much less restricted terms than in the past, provided that the borrower was relatively well-off. Although Luther initially sought to reverse this liberalising trend and outlaw usury altogether, Melanchthon broadly agreed with Eck in this and indeed amplified upon Eck's position. Calvin went even further, setting out, instead of the traditional limited set of circumstances under which usury was permitted, a restricted set of seven circumstances under which usury was sinful.

- In areas under Calvinist influence, such as the UK and Switzerland, Calvin rapidly came to be regarded as condoning practically all usury.

- The Catholics liberalised more gradually, still expressing strong reservations as late as *Rerum novarum,* published in the late nineteenth century.

- Another plank of objection to lending at interest arose particularly in the nineteenth century with the objection to "unearned income".

- Morally-driven restrictions on interest rates have been virtually non-existent in the UK for a long time. But usury laws persisted in many US states until 1981 (collapsing after a 1979 ruling that such laws applied in the state from which credit was supplied, not to transactions with residents of the state in question if supplied from another state). A number of EU Member States still have such laws even today.

79

Our purpose here is not to revisit this history in detail, but to reflect upon a couple of the key ancient arguments before moving on to interpret more recent events in their light.

Two ancient objections to usury

The most famous ancient objections to usury were from Aristotle. We shall consider just one: the argument that usury involves a conceptual error because metal is not fruitful. To understand this argument, we should consider how lending might take place in the absence of a metallic medium of exchange (e.g. gold). A farmer might borrow some seed, then plant it, and if the planting were fruitful the farmer might, say, have 30 or 100 times as much seed at the end as the amount borrowed. Then he could repay the loan, including some excess, allowing the lender to share in the fruitfulness of the project.

Aristotle contended that this was the correct concept of lending at interest. But gold is barren – it cannot be planted to produce more gold. So the borrower of gold cannot make gold grow, and hence charging interest on gold is confused. Many a thinker has been tempted to reject this argument outright. The Christian may think of the Parable of the Talents – doesn't the man with ten talents invest them wisely so as to produce ten more? Surely money *can* grow! Isn't the money just a proxy for some real goods, with those real goods able to be put to productive use and give rise to more real goods? Isn't Aristotle confusing the intrinsic value of a medium of exchange for the real product for which it stands?

In my view, whilst there is something in these objections, Aristotle has a more powerful point than such critics really engage with. For suppose that the following happens. Suppose that I borrow some gold, use it to buy seed, plant that seed, and produce a harvest of 30 or 100 times the amount I began with. Now, whereas before, when I borrowed the seed directly, under this scenario I would certainly have more of what I borrowed at the end than I did at the beginning, in the case of metallic borrowing this is no longer so. For the gold price of seeds might fall between when I buy the seeds and when I

80

garner my harvest. If that gold price falls far enough, then even if my project is fruitful in seed terms, it might not be fruitful in gold terms. Compared with lending real items, money lending at interest exposes the borrower to the risk of fluctuations in the money price of what he needs and what he produces. One (perhaps poor) way to express this point is to say that money is not *intrinsically* fruitful.

Now, a rich person might be able to diversify his risks such that the added risk of money borrowing is not relevant, but the same might not be true of a poor borrower. If we are to shield the poor borrower from such price fluctuation risk, we will need to express our lending to him more directly in terms of the underlying output (e.g. by buying shares in his project, rather than lending at interest).

The other argument we shall consider is that of Cato and Seneca. According to them, usury was akin to murder, because the usurer, like the murderer, took away a portion of a man's life. In the modern context, such a claim seems hysterical, but let us focus on a variant that the modern mind might find more appealing, as follows.

Many people of a libertarian bent object to any notion of a restriction on lending at interest. They would point out that, if the contract is entered into freely by both parties, they consider it to their mutual benefit, so (setting aside issues of the exploitation of monopoly power, a matter on which libertarians differ) it is counterproductive for anyone to try to prevent such a transaction.

This argument has a superficial attraction, until one reflects on the fact that we do not accept it across a number of other settings not terribly distant, conceptually, from lending at interest. Consider, for example, selling oneself into slavery. Doubtless there are libertarians that would say that such a transaction, if entered into freely, is perfectly legitimate. But few of the rest of us agree. Most of us take the view that some transactions involve people consenting to bear sufficiently unpleasant consequences that we do not permit them. The point here is not restricted to distaste merely for this precise transaction. For example, we would not accept people offering their own or their families' liberties as collateral on a loan (a common practice in the past).

This seems to me to be precisely the sort of issue under consideration in much anti-usury debate. The question is whether the terms of the loan involve such unpleasant consequences (presumably for the borrower) that we are not prepared to tolerate such a transaction even if the borrower would choose it freely for himself.

Now we see the analogy with Cato and Seneca's position. For the borrower subject to high interest rates may be committing himself to surrendering a large portion of his labour for a long period of his life in exchange for a modest loan. Is it really right for the lender to agree to do this, even if the borrower seeks it?

Modern issues

There are particular modern forms of high-interest lending that present other kinds of issues. For example, very short-term lending may predominate under conditions when borrowers have other high debts and are already insolvent, and the final loans may regularly presage bankruptcy. Under such conditions, the high interest short-term lender is siphoning off assets that the borrower is aware are already probably lost to him, at the expense of other creditors that might use those assets to recover some of their debts.

Such issues are interesting and important, but let us focus upon our older usury theme. There seems to me to be at least one potential application here that challenges a standard outlook that suggests that there should be no restraint on freely entered financial contracts. Specifically, is it proper for lenders to provide funds in settings where default by borrowers is likely? At first glance, there seems little in this thought. For is it not the lender that suffers if its loan is not repaid? If the lender is prepared to bear such losses, why is that any kind of matter for regulatory interest?

Well, the answer might be that it is not merely the lender that suffers. For a consequence of defaulting might be that the borrower loses access to credit in the future, and in modern society someone without access to credit may become excluded from many commercial transactions and thereby reduced in full participation in society. Thinking of this sort appears to be at least partly behind government proposals in 2009 that lenders should have a duty to investigate properly whether borrowers are well-placed to repay mortgages.

My view

My own view on this matter is that there is certainly a worthy challenge here, and if the circumstances of the borrower really were diminished sufficiently by default (or if borrowers were unable to default, but instead pursued indefinitely for loans they were unable to service) then there would be a strong case for considering the classical Catholic or at least Calvinist restrictions on usury. There probably are countries in the world today to which this is still relevant. This is perhaps also relevant in the case of illegal money-lending in the UK and (more commonly) in countries such as Germany (where illegal high-interest money lending is more common than in the UK because of German restrictions on legal high-interest lending).

However, it seems to me to be a mistake to believe that the degree of social exclusion created by losing access to credit really represents any serious analogy with enslavement in countries such as the UK, with well-established bankruptcy rules and social safety nets that provide cover against poverty in the material sense, at least in cases of legal money-lending.

I acknowledge, though, that this contention is intimately bound up with my concept of poverty, and in particular my view that in the moral sense poverty should be thought of in at least a "moving absolute" sense, rather than in terms of "relative poverty". In other words, my view is that what constitutes poverty is a matter of material deprivation, rather than inequality, but that the relevant concept of material deprivation shifts through time (for example, a family would count as in poverty today if the daughters of the household had to travel to the well twice a day and physically carry home water, even if in the Middle Ages it would have been a sign of affluence to have one's own well). Someone taking a different view from my own on what constitutes poverty (in particular, someone with a belief that poverty should be defined in terms of somebody's income – or consumption – relative to the average in society) might well conclude that there is more of a moral problem than I would allow with drawing people into the social exclusion associated with a loss of access to credit.

The above point about the views taken by others is of particular relevance in a democratic and integrated society. For I believe it is fairly clear that governments do not share my view about how much it is acceptable for the circumstances of borrowers to fall as a consequence of default, and they are even less willing to see the circumstances of lenders reduced by default. So an overly relaxed attitude to this moral aspect of usury is likely, in a democratic state, to result in government intervention to limit losses associated with default, with morally disastrous consequences we shall discuss below.

Building upon the above concerns, I believe that some of the traditional philosophical and Christian concerns about usury deserve much more prominence. In particular, although there may be limited, if any, case for legal or regulatory restriction upon lending even to those that might default, given that our social safety net prevents the bankrupt from falling so far into poverty as to make the Senecan analogies with slavery and murder apposite, it does not follow from this that we should feel no *moral* discomfiture in lending to those that might bankrupt themselves or appear likely to be taking on highly ill-advised loans that would place heavy burdens on them for long period. I suspect that this is a matter about which Christian moralists have been too relaxed for too long, and there could well be a case for looking much more closely at lessons from, for example, the growth in Islamic finance. Perhaps there should be "Christian finance", which does involve some lending at interest but where such lending does not occur in circumstances in which it would be immoral, and may involve more use of equity financing than would occur in secular models.

Furthermore, and as an aside, I also believe that some of the technical issues (such as the siphoning off of the assets of the insolvent, to the detriment of other creditors) might well be proper subjects of close scrutiny and even, potentially, regulation. Indeed, it is not inconceivable that, in a common law tradition, the courts may regard such transactions as unenforceable, if the circumstances of the borrower were known to the lender, as the lender is laying claim to assets which should already be earmakred for another creditor.

BAILOUTS

Regarding, bailouts, I shall state straight away that I consider the bailouts of banks and depositors in the financial crisis to be extremely immoral. The two most important reasons are:

- That we have used the wealth of ordinary working people (taxpayers) to bail out rich people who had made mistakes.

- That we have applied a different standard in dealing with systemic issues in respect of the banks and the wealthy people associated with them from that we applied when dealing with less wealthy people in less wealthy regions when dealing with mines, shipbuilding, car manufacturing and other industries of the 1970s and 1980s.

Bailing out the foolish rich

Intrinsically, what has happened is that we have taken a set of people that were amongst the richest in our society (those with so much wealth that they held large sums on deposit in banks and those with pensions – pension funds being major holders of bank shares) and transferred money to them from those that were not so rich. This happened when the investments of the rich turned bad in such a way that, had the transfer not happened, there would have been a re-ordering of the wealth in society. The group of people from whom we have transferred wealth include today's taxpayers in general but also tomorrow's taxpayers.

I understand, and do not deny, that there might have been a number of people in reduced circumstances if their pensions had to be reduced or if some portion of their bank deposits were lost. But that is what happens when investments go bad. A key part of the classical defence of wealthy people gaining "unearned income" from their wealth has always been that such "unearned income" was the fruit of investment. If there was no risk, there was no investment, and if there was no investment, why should these people be able to earn returns on their wealth? As we have seen, a key plank of the defence of lending at interest has always been that returns reflected risks taken. If no risk was taken, why was it legitimate for positive real interest to be paid?

Why are systemic issues more important for banks and Southern England than for mines and South Wales?

Now, of course, those advocating government bailouts of the banks contended that it was not about helping the rich, but, rather, preventing terrible depression with all the consequences that would have for the poor as well as the rich. But this was not a standard we have applied in the recent past in considering bailouts of less affluent people with impacts on less affluent areas.

When, in the 1970s and 1980s and 1990s, we closed down mines, and whole regions suffered from blight for decades, with many businesses collapsing as second round consequences of the loss of mines; or when similar things (albeit on a smaller scale) happened with the closure of shipyards or car factories, the argument was that such "systemic spillovers" were prices that had to be paid in order to allow markets to function, promoting efficiency, modernisation, innovation, and growth.

But in 2008, when it was not miners or shipbuilders but bankers, and not communities in the North-East or Scotland or Northern Ireland or Wales but instead the South-East and the wider country, we suddenly decided that systemic issues were extremely important. I believe that this seriously impairs the ability of governments to apply market disciplines to others in the future, at the very least until this bailout of the rich has been reversed and even then only by those that disavow the bailout.

Wider moral problems

Similarly, I feel that society is now in a very difficult moral position in respect of issues such as social security benefits or in considering the morality or otherwise of high taxes and progressive taxes. The usually moral arguments against high taxation and against progressive taxation have much less strength in an environment in which high earners in the finance sector and people with significant interest-earning wealth have been bailed out using government debt. This government debt must be repaid with future taxes. Who should pay these taxes – ordinary working people, or the high earners and those with high interest-earning wealth? The moral case for taxing the latter appears very strong. *"You and your kind received trillions to bail you out! How can you argue, in seriousness, against your paying higher taxes to pay for it!?"*

Similarly, why should society pay any attention to anyone with large bank deposits, bailed out at the taxpayer's expense, complaining about welfare benefits being overly generous or the moral hazard for the unemployed who may lack incentives to find work? *"You and your kind received trillions to bail you out! How can you argue, in seriousness, against a few pounds being used to assist a poor person!?"*

Issues of inefficiency in the economy arise all the time, as new technologies undercut the previous generation of semi-skilled workers, or international trade increases competition for labour from those in poorer countries. But when workers in inefficient industries come to the state in future asking for subsidies, on what basis are we to deny such subsidies to them? Obviously nothing to do with the cleansing necessity of change through market forces – we did not apply that reasoning to the banks, so we obviously don't believe in it. *"You and your kind received trillions to bail you out! How can you argue, in seriousness, against a pittance in subsidies being used to assist a postman, car worker and so on?"*

The arguments against social security benefits that create moral hazard or against bailing out declining industries have changed. Some will argue consistently against moral hazard and bailouts across all sectors of the economy. However, there is no doubt that the sound case that they make will gain less traction in policy circles because of the bailout of the banks.[1]

CONCLUSION

The failure of Christian moralists to give sufficient prominence to issues around usury and the consequent lack of a sufficiently robust account of how the possibility of *loss* is central to the entitlement to receive interest – whether through bank deposits or other forms of interest – has left governments and wider society operating in moral confusion when they faced circumstances such as those in the run-up to and aftermath of the credit crunch. The near-term consequences have been morally lax borrowing, morally empty lending and morally disastrous bailouts. The long-term consequences represent a serious threat to the moral support for free markets. It is simply morally unacceptable for market disciplines to be applied to the poor but not to the rich, and to borrowers but not to lenders.

Christians need to re-think these matters from scratch. Their contribution to the debate is urgently required. In the absence of such a contribution, the field will be left open to enemies of markets and the enemies of Christianity.

NOTE

1　It should be added that some economists do argue against bailouts whilst suggesting that the functions of failed financial institutions can still carry on so that there is no need to have a collapse of the bank payments system when banks become insolvent. As such, the spillover effects of the bank failing could be less than we suppose in any case.

CHRISTIAN PERSPECTIVES ON CONSUMER DEBT

BRIAN GRIFFITHS
Member of the House of Lords

———

In recent years, consumer debt has become an important issue in the UK. One reason is the sheer scale of the problem. The growth of consumer debt relative to household income over the past three decades has been enormous. In the mid-1970s the ratio of consumer debt to household income was roughly 40-50%. By 1995 it had reached 100% and by 2008 170%. Since 1992 debt grew during a period in which there were over sixty-four quarters of consecutive economic growth, low interest rates, rising house prices, low inflation and full-employment. By contrast, the financial crisis has meant falling income, rising unemployment, a lack of affordable housing, an inability to borrow and, at the same time, banks demanding repayment of existing loans. The result is that millions of households are struggling to repay debt.

Another reason is the nature of the problem: being over indebted produces serious personal and social problems ranging from stress to the break up of relationships, ill health, sick leave, mental health problems, depression and even suicide; it leads to repossessions of homes and personal bankruptcies. Individuals with debt problems are vulnerable to being charged high interest rates whether through credit cards or doorstep lending. In the case of the latter, critics cite examples of interest rates of over 100%. Worse still, if people need credit and if credit is difficult to obtain, people will resort to borrow from loan sharks.

Finally, debt is a particular problem for low income families excluded from the mainstream financial sector. Typically low income families are in receipt of welfare benefits, live in socially rented accommodation and are lone parents.

Because they have little savings to fall back on they are more vulnerable than other groups to the financial crisis.

Apart from these concerns the growth of consumer debt raises particular questions for Christians. Is the charging of interest ever justified on moral grounds? If it is, why did the church ban it for fifteen centuries? And why did the UK introduce Usury Laws? How should people who are struggling with debt be protected? Should the government do more to encourage mutual institutions to provide credit? How can the church help people in difficulty? Does the growth of debt reflect the values of a materialistic culture? What should be a Christian's attitude to their personal debt?

This chapter explores some of these questions and is divided into three sections: first it explores the Biblical background and seeks to draw out from it certain Christian principles; next, it examines issues of public policy in the light of the principles; and finally it looks briefly at issues for the church and for Christians.

THE HEBREW BIBLE AND THE NEW TESTAMENT

The basis of Christian teaching on debt and interest or usury comes from the Pentateuch. The Torah recognises that people who find themselves in economic difficulty may need to borrow; being in debt is never condemned as such. Small farmers in a simple agricultural community could find themselves having financial problems simply because of a bad harvest, raids on their cattle, the loss of family members or extortionate pricing. While the need to borrow is fully recognised, charging interest on loans to fellow Israelites was forbidden:

> "If you lend money to one of my people who is needy, do not be like a money lender; charge him no interest." (Ex 22:25)

> "If one of your countrymen becomes poor and is unable to support himself among you, help him as you would an alien or a temporary resident, so that he can continue

to live among you. Do not take interest of any kind from him… You must not lend him money at interest or sell him food at a profit." (Lev 25:35-37)

The injunction not to charge interest on a loan is again repeated in Deuteronomy (Deut 23:19, 20) but with the additional clause that interest may be charged to a foreigner but not to a brother Israelite.

The same themes occur throughout the Old Testament. King David in Psalm 15 states that would-be citizens of Zion should lend money without usury (Ps 15:5). Jeremiah lamented because he was treated as a usurer falsely (Jer 15:10). In the catalogue of sins prevailing in Jerusalem, Ezekiel lists usury and extortion (Ezek 22:12). When Nehemiah is rebuilding the walls of Jerusalem he rebukes those who have been charging interest and insists they repay their ill-gotten gains (Neh 5:9-12). Proverbs 22:7 states that "the borrower is servant to the lender" which suggests an unlevel playing field between the two.

There were three reasons for the ban on usury within the Jewish community. The first is that it protected the borrower. In Old Testament references to usury the borrower is typically poor or needy. Credit markets at the time were highly localised and personal, so that the potential for abuse through charging excessively high interest rates and imposing harsh terms on contracts was considerable. The ban on usury was therefore an early form of consumer protection. Next the ban on usury was a constraint on the growth of inequality in the distribution of income. It was one among a number of measures which prevented the growth of a wealthy class alongside the creation of an underclass.

Third, it had one objective which would not have been true of comparable legislation in other societies such as in Egypt, Phoenicia, Babylon, Greece, Mesopotamia and Assyria. Persons in need who wished to borrow were "brother Israelites", whom God describes as "one of my people". They were part of a nation which was unique because of its covenant with God and the ban on usury was a tangible symbol of a continuing covenant.

Aristotle's idea that money is barren was wholly alien to Jewish thought. The reasons given in the Old Testament for a ban on charging interest on loans to fellow Jews were intensely practical; by contrast Aristotle's notion was simply intellectual speculation. Nevertheless it was the basis on which the Third Lateran Council of the Church in 1179 condemned the practice as unlawful. Christians in various campaigning groups today who argue against the charging of interest and wish to place ceilings on interest rates are much closer to the Greek tradition of rationalism than to Hebrew thought.

When we come to the New Testament, there is a continuity between the teaching of the Gospels and Jewish Law. Jesus taught that the whole of the law and the prophets could be summed up in two precepts: "You shall love the Lord your God with all your heart, with all your soul and with all your mind. And its second like is, you shall love your neighbour as yourself" (Mt 22:37-39).

In the context of usury Jesus emphasised the importance of generosity. He taught his followers that to love your neighbour as yourself meant lending without the expectation of any return.

> "And if you lend to those from whom you expect repayment, what credit is that to you? Even 'sinners' lend to 'sinners', expecting to be repaid in full. But love your enemies, do good to them and lend to them without expecting to get anything back. Then your reward will be great and you will be sons of the most high because he is kind to the ungrateful and wicked." (Lk 6:34-35)

Generosity is a core value of the Kingdom he came to establish. Jesus does not set out an economic programme but in two of his parables, that of the pounds (Lk 19:11-27) and that of the talents (Mt 25:14-30), he acknowledges the value of interest earned on deposit and the value of profits from shrewd investment.

From this teaching a number of principles emerge: One is the social value of credit and credit markets. Borrowing and lending are a natural part of economic life and without credit markets people would suffer. In the UK, mainstream credit markets are highly competitive and valued by those who borrow and lend. Credit markets enable people to smooth out their consumption over a lifetime, typically by obtaining a mortgage on a property in early working life and then repaying it in later life. They also allow people to borrow if they have specific requirements such as for school and college fees, costs of re-training and home improvement.

Second, this teaching recognises the toxic potential of personal debt. The fact that "the borrower is servant to the lender" suggests that in credit markets the borrower is typically more vulnerable than the lender. The playing field is not level. In extreme circumstances lenders can exploit the vulnerability of the borrowers by charging exorbitant interest rates and imposing conditions on the terms of loans which are hard.

Third, borrowers need protection. In an embedded economy such as the Old Testament in which economic activity was within and between families and conducted on the basis of trust and sharing, charging interest on loans was forbidden. Even though usury was banned it was not a sin comparable to that of murder, theft or adultery. It was not condemned in the Ten Commandments. It was perfectly legitimate for a person to charge interest to a foreigner, who would have been part of a much larger and more competitive market place.

Fourth, there is the importance of generosity. Jesus' whole life was lived for others. The model for his leadership was that of a servant. As he watched rich people putting their money into the Temple treasury he said that they gave out of their wealth, but a poor widow was praised who gave only two mites because she had given everything she possessed.

Finally Jesus, in His teaching, speaks out against materialism and the worship of money. He was not opposed to the material world. He worked as a craftsman contributing to wealth creation. He enjoyed being entertained by friends and followers. He was equally convinced however that "man does not live by bread alone". More than that He warned against the temptations of money and wealth. He said that it was harder for a camel, the largest known animal, to go through the eye of a needle, the smallest known aperture, than for a rich person to enter the Kingdom of God. He personified and deified money, calling it Mammon, and making it clear that it was impossible to serve God and Mammon.

FOUR ISSUES OF PUBLIC POLICY

At the beginning of this chapter we argued that consumer debt had become an important issue in the UK for a number of reasons. The principles which emerge from Judaeo-Christian teaching provides us with guidelines for tackling current problems associated with debt, of which four are important.

Competition issues

One objective of public policy should be to ensure that markets for credit are competitive. For the majority of borrowers competitive markets are the best way of providing access to credit products. Consumers will be best served and given greater choice by ensuring freedom of entry into credit markets, reducing the size of barriers to entry to the lowest possible, breaking up existing cartels or price agreements and ensuring that market abuse through market dominance by any one institution is tackled. Competition will deliver the lowest possible interest rate levels, given the level of risk, and improved levels of service and innovation in new products. The markets for prime lending (mortgages, credit cards, hire purchase) were highly competitive and highly innovative before the financial crisis.

The financial crisis has resulted in a reduction in the number of firms in the industry: Alliance and Leicester and the deposits of Bradford and Bingley were bought by Santander; Lloyds merged with HBOS; and there has been consolidation in the number of building societies, associated with Nationwide and the merger of Britannia and the Co-op. A reduction in the number of firms in the sector raises questions over whether competition has been reduced. While banks re-build their capital, the cost of mortgages has risen and, even at higher rates of interest, their availability has been reduced. The difficulty of obtaining credit in order to reschedule existing debt means that more people are confronted with default, repossession and insolvency.

The area of consumer credit where the problem of competition is greatest is in sub-prime lending which covers doorstep lending and rent-to-own stores and which includes products such as pay-day loans, auto-title loans and sale and buy-back. In the market for home credit, one company had 50% market share and the largest four companies together had 70%, a complaint was lodged against the industry on the basis that firms had a limited incentive to compete on price or to attempt to get business by taking over other lenders' loans.

The Competition Commission reported in November 2006 and found that the industry was making excess profits of £75million per year as a result of a lack of effective price competition. The Commission proposed a package of remedies requiring lenders to share data on customer payment records, publish prices on a website so that customers could compare charges, require lenders to provide more public information about the product and ensure that those who repay loans early get a fair rebate. Since then the third largest doorstep lender, London Scottish Bank, has gone into administration, so competition is now further reduced. In the last recession of 1990/1991 the demand for sub-prime borrowing increased as potential borrowers were unable to obtain credit from prime lenders and in the current crisis it seems that the demand for sub-prime lending is increasing while the supply of credit in this area is being reduced.

Arguably the most serious danger of all is that people who cannot otherwise obtain credit will turn to illegal money lenders and loan sharks. Research commissioned by the DTI (the predecessor of BERR) concluded that there are approximately 165,000 households borrowing from illegal money lenders in the UK, which accounts for 6% of households in the most deprived areas and roughly 3% of low income households overall. The department launched pilots to analyse illegal money lending in Birmingham and Glasgow, found close links between illegal lending, violence, intimidation and extortion and have been successful in identifying loan sharks as well as making prosecutions.

One approach which has been explored in the US in dealing with the middle ground between prime lending and illegal loan sharks is the attempt to define predatory lending legally. This would cover areas in which lenders provided limited information to borrowers, targeted a particularly vulnerable class of person or knowingly sold over-priced loans to people whose mental and physical status made them vulnerable to face-to-face selling. One proposed definition of predatory lending is:

> "Intentionally placing consumers in loan products with significantly worse terms and/or higher costs than loans offered to similarly qualified customers in the region, for the primary purpose of enriching the originator and with little or no regard for the costs to the consumer."

The problems with this approach are twofold. It is difficult to give precision to the phrase "significantly worse terms" and it is also difficult to discern the lender's state of mind. Various other definitions have been offered but all suffer from the same defects. Certain states in the US have introduced these laws but the problem is that they tend to catch legitimate lending at high interest rates which are high because of the risk associated with the borrowers and the costs of debt collection and so they end up reducing the supply of credit more than is desirable.

Community finance initiative and credit unions

One area which public policy is addressing but in which more can and should be done is that of increasing the provision of credit for low income families through alternative sources of credit, such as credit unions and community finance initiatives which are a legacy of the co-operative and self-help movement that originated in Britain in the nineteenth century.

Credit unions have been much more successful in Ireland, Australia, the Caribbean and the US than they have been in the UK. They are basically financial co-operatives owned and run by and for their members and joined together by a

96

common bond such as employment in the same company or organisation or residence in the same area. Credit unions have two objectives, to encourage saving and to provide access to low-cost credit for people on low incomes.

Until recently credit unions were restricted in the interest rates they could charge, the nature of the common bond they could choose, the repayment methods they could require and in their saving requirements. As a result of this they lacked scale and found it difficult to attract the best management. More recently the government introduced a reform order for credit unions and industrial and provident societies which will make the consumer bond less onerous in terms of attracting members; make it profitable for groups as well as individuals to become members; allow credit unions to pay interest on deposits; enable credit unions to charge market rates for services; publish unaudited interim accounts; and remove the statutory limit on non-qualifying members. They have also introduced the Co-operative and Community Benefit Societies and Credit Unions Bill to help the sector.

These are all moves in the right direction. The only question is whether they are enough. At present there is a lack of scale in the credit union movement which requires pump-priming to enable it to increase the professionalism of its management and introduce systems to compete more effectively with retail banks. In 2005 credit unions lent £353million while doorstep lenders extended new loans of £1.5billion. To reach a critical scale, the Treasury needs to finance a series of pilots to determine whether credit unions and community finance initiatives have the potential to be viable financially and to reach sufficient scale to compete with existing providers. It would not however be appropriate for them to be funded permanently by taxpayers' money.

Disclosure and transparency in banks

Prime lenders have come in for strong criticism for a number of their lending practices: the charge is that it has become too easy to obtain credit; their marketing is too aggressive; the terms on which credit is given are not fully known; bank branches have become money shops concerned with selling credit rather than offering impartial advice; and, because technology has replaced people, the process of lending has become an impersonal business. Certain of these criticisms have been set out in detail in two reports issued by the House of Commons Treasury Select Committee. The lack of transparency relates to the information provided regarding interest free periods, administration charges, minimum repayment requirements, and penalty charges, such as for late payment and exceeding credit limits. It has also been argued that the sheer complexity and small print associated with many products, means that it is difficult for people to understand what they are buying or easy to buy the wrong product.

In recent years the government has taken a number of steps to improve disclosure and transparency for which it deserves credit, but as the government itself says "there is further to go" (Reforming Financial Models. CM 7667.8.25.P.107). More could be done to improve the transparency of financial products, to curb over-aggressive selling techniques and to require lenders to take due care in lending. In July 2007, the government published a White Paper on 'A Better Deal for Consumers' which includes a review of credit cards and store cards, unsolicited credit card cheques and due care in lending and, at the same time, the Office of Fair Trading announced a review of high cost credit which will look at markets such as doorstep lending and pay-day loans where the typical APR is 50% or more.

Should interest rates be capped?

As a result of the high costs of sub-prime credit, various organizations have called for the imposition of an interest rate ceiling to be placed on loans, so that it would be illegal for lenders to charge an interest rate higher than the set ceiling. Such policies are in place in Germany, France and Ireland; and in the UK credit unions are subject to an interest rate cap.

There are several reasons, however, why capping interest rates is a bad idea.

Firstly, the government would have to specify in great detail exactly what could and could not be included in the APR calculation. This would invite the home credit industry to develop ingenious devices to get around the official restrictions. For example in Germany the transaction costs for purchase are included in the APR, but a range of other routine costs (cash withdrawals, statement fees, correspondence fees) are not included. In the US, exemptions are typically provided for pawnbrokers and auto loans but not for others. Indeed, the high costs of collection of sub-prime loans, where home visits are often used to collect debts on a weekly basis, means that there are many elements of the repayment that do not comprise interest at all.

Secondly, if the ceilings were introduced in this way, and at the levels which have been suggested, it would kill the home credit industry. For decades in the UK, rent control killed the private rented sector in housing, but it did not kill off housing demand. In fact the opposite was true: it increased it. Exactly the same would be true in this market. Research conducted for the former Department of Trade and Industry on this subject concluded that 'In markets where rate ceilings are introduced ... if the business model and pricing structures cannot be adapted to fit within the new framework, lenders tend to withdraw from the market'. In 2000 the State of Florida imposed rate ceilings on Auto Title lenders, who provided high cost short-term cash credit to largely unbanked car owners. Twelve months later the number of lenders had dropped from 600 to 58. Indeed, one might consider whether the interest rate cap that applies to credit unions prevents more effective competition in this market.

Thirdly, if there is an excess demand for sub-prime consumer credit at the capped interest rates, illegal lenders will step in to fill the gap. Evidence suggests there is significantly more illegal lending in both France and Germany than in the UK. In the UK, 3% of those who are on low incomes and who are credit-impaired are prepared to admit they have borrowed from an illegal lender. In France this figure is 7% and in Germany 8%.

Fourthly, the consumers most affected by interest rate caps would be the most vulnerable, unbanked, credit-impaired, low income individuals and families in the country. Those on low incomes who have been refused loans in the UK are estimated to be roughly 4%. In Germany this figure is put at 10% and in France 12%.

Finally, price transparency would appear to be compromised when ceilings are introduced. One of the characteristics of a significant minority of low income borrowers is that they have regular late and missed payments. Because in these instances extra charges are imposed, the interest rate frequently does not reflect true cost of credit, as noted above.

THE CHURCH AND PROBLEMS OF DEBT

The problems faced by people struggling with debt typically follow a well defined route. The initial trigger for developing a problem is usually an unexpected change in circumstances such as redundancy, long-term sick leave, ill-health, the loss of existing overtime or bonus payments or the break up of a relationship. The first symptom of a downward debt spiral is typically a missed payment which could well result in a penalty charge. The next step is that borrowers then attempt to juggle their finances to prioritise the payment of one debt over another by, for example, repaying credit card debt by not paying council tax or not paying utility bills. This is followed by pressure from creditors whether through telephone calls at work or visits to the home, typically in the early morning or late evening.

The pressure of escalating debt and harassment from debt collectors leads to denial, emotional stress and personal financial chaos. Creditors may then advise them to borrow from other lending institutions or from family or friends in order to repay the debt. If payments are not forthcoming the next step is legal proceedings, enforcement orders, bankruptcy and repossession. At the end there may be total financial loss or even mental breakdown and, in extreme cases, suicide. These steps in the debt spiral are drawn from the experiences of hundreds of debt advisers who have worked with thousands of different clients of varying income backgrounds in widely differing organisations and all regions of the UK. The Church and Christian people are involved in many such charities trying to help people resolve their difficulties.

Research conducted by Citizens Advice have found that the present financial crisis has resulted in significant worsening of debt problems for individuals and families. Debt enquiries have doubled over the last ten years and debt is now the number one issue with which they deal. It accounts for one in three of all enquiries. A survey conducted from analysed data from over 1,400 debt clients which was published in a report, *A Life in Debt*, showed that more than 20% of their clients were lone parents and the reasons they gave for having debt problems were low income, irresponsible lending, badly informed financial decisions and unreasonable debt collection practices. Typical comments were "we over extended ourselves by remortgaging", "I had easy access to credit", "credit was pushed at me – I was given new loans to consolidate or pay off my debts", "I didn't understand the credit terms. I owe £12,000 for a £3,000 television set."

These problems present an enormous opportunity for the church. People in debt need someone to listen, give practical advice, help them restructure their finances and then help them get back on an even keel. The crisis has seen a growth in debt counselling by churches and faith-based organisations. From the perspective of our society and of people outside the church this is where the rubber hits the road, and it takes time and money. The Church must teach the virtue of prudence so that people are less likely to get into trouble in the first place. The teaching of prudence – including the use of income to pay down debts or to put aside money for a 'rainy day' – is not something just for times of crisis when the problems of debt are in the front of our minds. Prudence is a virtue to be practised week in, week out, particularly when times are favourable.

CHRISTIAN PERSPECTIVES ON THE FINANCIAL CRISIS – THE ROLE OF CREDIT UNIONS

MICK McATEER

Director, The Financial Inclusion Centre

INTRODUCTION

The perfect financial storm that has recently battered the UK and Western economies has been described by some commentators as the most serious financial crisis the global financial system has faced since the First World War.

Policymakers and regulators have embarked on an unprecedented range of interventions including: improving deposit protection schemes to protect consumers' savings; the de facto nationalisation of a number of the UK's major banks; massive injections of public funds into the banking system; dramatic cuts in benchmark interest rates; a programme of quantitative easing by the Bank of England; and the establishment of an Asset Protection Scheme (APS) to offer banks insurance against future risks and losses.

So far, the UK authorities (Government, Bank of England and Financial Services Authority) and their European and international counterparts have understandably prioritised the rescue and stabilisation of the financial system. While complacency must be avoided due to the risk of a further banking crisis, these interventions by policymakers do seem to have been successful in rescuing and stabilising the banking and financial system.

However, we must not forget how the financial crisis and subsequent and consequent recession has affected the most vulnerable consumers. Increasing numbers of vulnerable communities will become exposed to predatory lending practices by sub-prime lenders and loan sharks, and financial scams.

Moreover, the effects will not be short term in nature and are likely to be felt for a decade, if not a generation. A major restructuring of the financial services industry is currently underway. The combination of regulatory and commercial pressures means that 'mainstream' financial institutions are increasingly likely to concentrate on offering products and services to lower-risk, medium-higher income households. The increased use of risk-based pricing will exacerbate the chronic levels of financial exclusion facing the UK. Vulnerable consumers will find it increasingly difficult to obtain access to fair, affordable and suitable products – particularly in the banking, credit and insurance sectors.

Now that Middle England has been protected, we need to devote just as much effort and resources to protecting the interests of financially excluded consumers. We need to reinvigorate the idea of mutually owned, community based financial institutions as an alternative to the mainstream financial services industry. One model of community based financial institutions that has been established in many countries around the world is the credit union.

WHAT IS A CREDIT UNION?

A credit union is a financial co-operative that is owned, controlled and run by its members. The main products they offer their members are access to savings accounts and low cost loans. Some of the larger credit unions offer a wider range of products and services such as current accounts which provide facilities such as ATM cards and direct debits.

The core essence of a credit union is the 'common bond'. The common bond determines who can join the credit union and become a member. As the name implies, members have to be bonded by some common factor such as living or working in the same area, working for the same employer, or membership of a church. This common bond structure is supposed to bind the members of the credit union together and promote collective responsibility and trust.

HOW DO CREDIT UNIONS WORK?

Credit unions work on a very simple model. The savings deposited by the credit union members provide a pool of funds which can then be used to make loans. Borrowers pay interest on their loans. From the interest received on loans, credit unions need to pay operating costs and make a surplus to put into reserves, develop the business and pay a dividend to savers – this is intended to attract further deposits.

Some credit unions can pay dividends that are comparatively attractive compared with mainstream financial institutions. According to ABCUL (the trade body)[1], typical dividends tend to be 2% or 3% on share deposits held. Although it should be stressed that many smaller credit unions especially in the earliest days may not be able to pay a dividend. In that case, it can help to have a large bank of 'ethical' savers who are not purely motivated by financial gains willing to support the credit union in the early days.

An interesting feature of credit unions is that life insurance is built in at no extra cost to the member. This means that on the death of a member the amount of savings held can be doubled and paid out to a beneficiary nominated by the member. Similarly, the insurance can be used to repay a loan on the death of a member.

While credit unions might not offer the very cheapest loan rates, they can be quite competitive and attractive especially for consumers who may not be offered loans by mainstream lenders and might be forced to turn to high cost sub-prime lenders or – even worse – loan sharks. Some credit unions charge around 1% a month on a reducing balance – this equates to an Annual Percentage Rate (APR) of 12.7%[2]. Many credit unions – again, smaller less established credit unions – will charge more for loans. However, the rates on credit union loans are capped by law and this means that they cannot charge more than 2% a month which equates to an APR of 26.8%.

It is useful to put this into context. The APR on a one-year £1,000 loan from a mainstream lender ranges from around 8%-19%. In contrast, if when consumers borrow from a home-credit company they can expect to be charged 122%-325% APR. For example, someone borrowing £300 for a year with Provident Financial (a home credit company) might expect to pay back £504 in total – an APR of 183%, whereas, with a typical credit union they might expect to pay back £321. Moreover, if borrowers need small, short term loans the APR can be eye-watering. The APR charged by home credit companies on a £100 loan over three months ranges from 600% APR to over 1,000% APR[3] Another growth area in the UK is payday loans. Payday loans are an idea imported from the USA and are intended to provide borrowers with a very short-term loan until the next wage is received. As with doorstep credit these loans are very expensive. The typical APR for borrowing £100 for one month from a payday lender is 1,290%.[4]

Case study

A case study from the ABCUL website illustrates how credit unions can help borrowers in difficulty to escape loan traps[5]. It refers to a lone parent living in Lewisham in London who took out a loan from the Provident for £700 who was expected to make 32 repayments of £35 under the terms of the loan – a total of £1,120. However, the total weekly household income was only £94 primarily made up of income support and child benefit. The cost of repaying the loan amounted to 37% of total household income.

The member approached the local credit union to see if they could help with the loan. The credit union assessed the application and approved the loan in this case. The credit union paid off the remainder of the Provident loan which amounted to £500. The member had to pay £10.25 a week over fifty-two weeks – a total of £533 (equal to an APR of 12.7%). Borrowing from the credit union saved the member over £350 in interest.

HOW CREDIT UNIONS ARE RUN

A key difference between a credit union and a commercial bank is the governance and accountability structures. Credit unions are managed and controlled by a volunteer board of executive and non-executive directors – in contrast to the well-paid professional directors that run banks. The officers who run the credit union are elected at the Annual General Meeting and all members have one vote regardless of the size of their savings.

The day-to-day running of the credit union may be done by staff and volunteers but the members – through their elected representatives – very much control the credit union. So, it could be argued that credit unions are much more democratic and accountable than larger, shareholder based financial institutions.

The role of volunteers from the local community must be recognised. Apart from the very largest credit unions which may have a number of full-time paid staff, most credit unions in the UK would not survive without the involvement of committed volunteers.

ARE CREDIT UNIONS SAFE?

Understandably, people may be under the impression that it is safer to deposit savings with a large bank rather than a small, local credit union. It must be said that many smaller credit unions will not have access to the same degree of professional skills and experience as a major bank. However, it is important to reassure potential members that credit unions come under the same consumer protection regime as banks and building societies.

Credit unions (and the officers that undertake the key functions) are authorised and regulated by the Financial Services Authority. Moreover, members' savings are protected by the Financial Services Compensation Scheme (FSCS) which provides 100% protection for the first £50,000 of their savings in the event of a credit union going under.

HOW CAN PEOPLE BECOME INVOLVED?

The more active, community spirited people get involved in making credit unions work, the better. If people are interested in becoming involved with credit unions they can do so in a number of ways.

They can volunteer in the local branch of an existing credit union, perhaps acting as a cashier or helping out with administration tasks or promoting and marketing the credit union. Credit unions would not survive without volunteers.

People should also think about becoming a director of an existing credit union. Credit union directors are also volunteers and do not get paid so it takes a degree of personal commitment to the credit union ideal. But it can be well worth it. People with enthusiasm, spare time, general skills and local knowledge of communities are always welcome. However, many credit unions would also benefit from directors with specialist experience and skills such as accountancy, marketing, human resources and so on. Credit unions may be community-based organisations run mainly by volunteers but they need to act with skill and integrity and they face many of the same complex technical, financial and regulatory issues as other larger financial institutions with far greater resources at their disposal.

However, involvement can be taken a stage further if individuals or groups of like-minded people in a local community or workplace take the initiative to set up a credit union in their local area. This is a not a step to be taken lightly. It requires stamina, a commitment to the credit union ethos, a desire to make a difference, and most importantly the dedication and perseverance to see it through. ABCUL reckons that it can take anywhere between one and three years to get a credit union up and running from the original idea.

Before going through the process of creating a credit union from scratch, the first thing to do is to check to see if there are credit unions in a neighbouring area who might consider expanding their common bond to cover other areas.

However, if the group concludes that there is a need to set up a new credit union then there are a number of stages that have to be completed. The key stages are: deciding on the common bond (see above); bringing together the people with the right mix of skills and experience; understanding the demand for services; developing a proper, realistic business plan; satisfying the FSA; and raising the necessary funding.

But people should not be fazed too much. ABCUL and other agencies such as local authorities will provide very useful assistance and in some cases financial resources to help new groups. Anyone who is interested in setting up a credit union can find details and helpful resources on the ABCUL website.[6]

THE HISTORY OF CREDIT UNIONS

Credit unions can be seen as part of the wider co-operative and mutual movement. The core ideas and values that define credit unions were developed in the nineteenth century. For example, it is possible to draw a link between modern credit unions and the work of pioneers such as Robert Owen in Britain, considered to be one of the founding fathers of the co-operative movement, Herman Schulze-Delitzsch and Frederick Wilhelm Raiffesen who were responsible for creating the first credit unions in Germany in 1852 and 1864, and Alphonse Desjardin in North America. The credit union movement grew quickly in North America and began to influence the rest of the world.

Credit unions in Jamaica started in the 1940s as a result of the efforts of a Jesuit priest, Fr John P. Sullivan, who believed that credit unions could help people cope with wartime conditions.

The first credit union in Ireland was founded in 1958 thanks to the work of schoolteacher Nora Herlihy and colleagues from the Dublin Central Co-operative Society. Credit unions are well established in Ireland as can be seen from the table, below. Moreover, credit unions in Northern Ireland were given a real boost by being part of a wider movement of civil rights and community associations.

For example, the Derry Credit Union in Northern Ireland has over 30,000 adult and junior members and is a rival for the big banks in Northern Ireland. It was formed in 1960 at a time when Derry was scarred by chronic, appalling levels of unemployment, deprivation and discrimination. Very few people in working class communities owned their own home to use as collateral which meant they had to turn to the notorious money lenders. The credit union met a very real financial exclusion need in one of the most deprived communities in Western Europe. But there is more to it than that. For citizens of the Creggan and Bogside areas of Derry in the 1960s and 1970s, the credit union was 'the people's bank', run by the people for the benefit of the community, while the struggle for financial self-sustainability seemed to be connected to the wider struggle for civil rights.

Credit unions have struggled – comparatively speaking – to make the same sort of impact in Great Britain, although real progress is being made. However, with the exception of a small number of communities, the same conditions that allowed credit unions to flourish in Ireland do not seem to exist to the same degree in Great Britain. If they are to make inroads into tackling financial exclusion, it is likely that significant state support and intervention will be needed to level the playing field for credit unions (see below).

FACTS AND FIGURES

There are some impressive statistics that attest to the potential for credit unions as a significant force for good in communities. As at end 2007, 49,000 credit unions with an estimated 177 million members had been established in ninety-six countries around the world.[7] Credit unions have over US$1 trillion in assets, nearly US$990 billion in savings, and nearly US$ 850 billion out on loan.[8]

Globally, the sector has achieved an average 'penetration rate' of 7.5%[9] of the economically active population. However, it must be pointed out that the global data disguise quite a variation in credit union success across regions (see Table below).

WORLDWIDE CREDIT UNION PENETRATION RATES
(DECEMBER 2007)

Region	Number of credit unions	Members (million)	Penetration rate
Africa	11,849	15	8.4%
Asia	20,199	33	2.6%
Caribbean	317	1.9	41%
Central Asia	387	0.1	0.26%
Europe	2,671	8.2	3.6%
Latin America	2,504	15	4.8%
Middle East	1,584	0.5	1%
North America	9,328	99	44%
Oceania	295	3.7	22%
Totals	**49,134**	**177**	**7.5%**

Even within regions, there is a significant variation in the importance of credit unions. For example, credit unions have been hugely successful in Ireland and account for just under 80% of the total assets held by European credit unions.[10]

CREDIT UNIONS IN BRITAIN

The credit union sector in Britain is making progress. According to the Financial Services Authority (FSA), 655,000 adults and 96,000 junior savers were members of British credit unions as at June 2008 – the total number of members at the end of 2000 amounted to only 325,000. The value of savings and loans has also shown significant growth. As at June 2008, savings with credit unions amounted to £475million compared to £183million at the end of 2000. Over the same period, loans increased from £175million to £429million.[11]

However, despite this rate of growth, credit unions are not yet a major force in Great Britain, and are a long way off being a significant rival for the big banks or even for the commercial sub-prime/home credit loan sector. Commercial sub-prime/home credit firms lent around £4.3 billion in 2005 which means that for every £1 credit unions have been lending, commercial providers lent out about £10.

The contrast with Ireland is stark. Credit unions in Ireland are considered to provide meaningful competition for the banks. It is estimated that around 50% of the population in Ireland belongs to a credit union, compared with around 1% of the population in Great Britain. Even within Great Britain, credit union presence tends to be concentrated in Scotland and urban English areas where there are large Irish and Caribbean communities.

The reasons for this lack of penetration in Great Britain are complex. But there are two overriding factors. Firstly, it needs to be recognised that a liberalised, market-based approach is ineffective at ensuring vulnerable consumers are treated fairly and have access to good value products and services in complex markets such as financial services. Expecting that credit unions will grow organically as a result of sovereign consumers exercising choice in a competitive market-based environment is a triumph of hope or ideology over experience. This could be addressed by robust intervention in the market to control the activities of commercial sub-prime lenders and a levelling of the playing field for not-for-profit community lenders such as credit unions. Secondly, it highlights the

111

need for extra resources to build capacity in the community lending sector to give it a chance to meet the need for fair and affordable credit.

Clearly, the credit union model works very well in some countries (as Ireland shows). But it is important to recognise the particular socio-economic conditions in which credit unions can thrive.

There are many very successful credit unions particularly in places like Ireland and Scotland. But the credit unions that have flourished – as well as being well-run financial institutions in their own right – seem to be in areas that have a real historical sense of community.

But we must avoid getting too romantic about community based lenders or the concept of self-help which seems to be flavour of the month at the moment. The sense of community and spirit of activism that exists in places such as Derry is very difficult to recreate in larger, fragmented urban areas. If the success of credit unions in Ireland and Scotland is to be replicated in the UK more resources need to be pumped into the sector to make them successful.

WHY ARE CREDIT UNIONS DIFFERENT?

On the face of it, credit unions and banks undertake the same role. Both types of institution intermediate savings (or investments) and turn them into loans – albeit on very different scales. However, in reality there are huge differences in structure, ethos and practices.

The most obvious difference is that banks are owned by external shareholders. Bank directors have a legal duty to maximise shareholders' interests under company law. Profits earned by the bank are returned to the shareholders directly in the form of dividends or through appreciation of the share price.

Of course, some bank customers may also be shareholders either directly or indirectly through pension or investment funds. However, shareholders and customers of banks are very much seen as separate groups of stakeholders whose distinct interests must be satisfied. According to the classical theories of free markets this should not matter as the dynamics provided by competition and consumer choice will work to align the interests of both sets of stakeholders. After all, as the theory goes, directors need to offer good value products and services and treat customers fairly to ensure the bank wins market share and delivers profit growth which, in turn, will result in profitability and share price appreciation to the benefit of shareholders.

However, we know from painful experience that competition and market forces in financial services have not been particularly effective at ensuring that customers are treated fairly or that banks deliver value – or perhaps competition itself is more limited than in other markets. The result is that directors incentivised by remuneration schemes linked to share price performance will strive to ensure that the shareholder interest takes precedence over the customer interest.

With the credit union model, the members are the owners and the customers. Any surplus (profit) made on the credit union's activities are retained to develop the credit union or pay dividends to members. It is easy to be sentimental about credit unions but they are not-for-profit organisations and in the main do seem to be driven by an ethos of service to their members, rather than maximising profit.

They are also seen by many consumers as an ethical way to bank, providing social benefits by tackling financial exclusion in deprived areas and providing a sense of community identity. Moreover, bank shares are predominantly owned by large institutional shareholders (or the state in the case of the rescued banks) which means that profits are not reinvested in local communities. The nature of credit unions, with the common bond and locally based operations, means that assets and surpluses are retained for use within the local area.

It is hard not to be struck by the view that the credit union model (along with some 'pure' building societies) remains closest to the original concept of retail banking in that access to sustainable loans is funded out of deposits from savers (rather than from wholesale funding markets, off-balance-sheet investments, or complex financial instruments such as securitised investment vehicles).

Moreover, banks and other lenders use sophisticated technology-based risk management techniques and credit rating models to assess the risk of a borrower repaying a loan. A common criticism of these risk-assessment techniques is that decision making on loans has become remote and automated. The authority of local community-based branch managers with the experience and discretion to make decisions based on first-hand knowledge of borrowers has been severely curtailed if not completely removed.

In contrast to the automated, remote world of corporate banking, credit unions still largely rely on first-hand know-ledge of borrowers and, through the existence of the 'common bond', pressure of responsibility to a group of fellow members to ensure that loans are repaid (that is the theory anyway).

THE ROLE OF CREDIT UNIONS IN A POST-CRISIS WORLD

With the right policy interventions, credit unions could be effective at helping with a number of key public policy objectives:

- protecting the most vulnerable in society from the effects of the financial crisis;
- maintaining access to affordable credit for vulnerable communities;
- promoting a savings/thrift culture and self-sufficiency; and
- tackling general financial exclusion in disadvantaged communities.

Looking at the ethos and commercial model of credit unions it would seem that these community based organisations are an idea whose time has come and seem ideally suited to filling the gaps left by high street/mainstream financial institutions to meet the needs of disadvantaged communities.

We need to alter the balance in the UK and encourage a savings and thrift culture and move away from a debt-fuelled culture of consumption. We do seem to have got the balance in the UK wrong, certainly in terms of our attitudes to saving and consumption and the balance of regulation.

At the time of the recent financial crisis, total personal debt in the UK reached £1.4 trillion – 155% of household disposable income. On the eve of the crisis, first time buyers were spending 34% of take home pay on mortgage payments – the highest since the eve of the previous housing crash in the early 1990s. First time buyers paid on average £40,000 more for their homes than they would have done if property prices had grown in line with long term trends – resulting in one of the greatest transfers of private wealth from one generation to another in modern times.[12] Older, middle-class households benefited hugely leaving younger generations with legacy debts which will take decades to unwind.

However, the UK household savings ratio is at its lowest for 50 years. Nearly half the population have savings of less than £1,500 – around one month's median earnings. Around a quarter have no savings at all – this figure rises to 62% of the poorest households.

The decade in the run up to the end of 2007 seems to have been a period of collective self-delusion, where we lost touch with reality, our thinking distorted by the drug of debt-financed property price growth.

There are many causes of the development of a "debt culture". Such causes might have included the liberalisation of retail mortgage and lending markets in the 1980s and 1990s; the growth in advertising-led consumerism; the development of lending markets which – in contrast to savings markets – were deregulated and liberalised; the erosion of a culture of thrift that had been passed down at least to the post-war generation; and loose monetary policy and low interest rates in the middle of the first decade of the twenty-first century.

Arguably, credit became commoditised and was aggressively sold and marketed. Consumer credit is a means to an end. When used positively, it allows consumers to meet a real, pressing financial need that cannot be met out of current income (perhaps because the consumer has suffered a temporary drop in disposable income). Affordable consumer credit can help consumers aspire to a better lifestyle that, rightly or wrongly, they feel they deserve. However, when abused, credit and its extreme version – over-indebtedness – can be downright dangerous.

Different consumer dynamics operate in the savings and loans markets. In contrast to savings, consumers will often be painfully aware that they need to borrow money – they know when there is a specific item of expenditure that needs to be covered by savings, current income or borrowing. If consumers are unable to cover these core needs from current income and/ or savings they may have no option but to turn to borrowing. They will therefore be well primed to seek out credit and, equally, be very vulnerable to aggressive selling of credit and predatory behaviour by sub-prime lenders and loan sharks.

It is always tempting to oversimplify in these cases but during the course of the runaway debt boom – right up to the eve of the crisis breaking – it seemed to be possible for a consumer to obtain a £5,000 loan in the space of five minutes, yet it would have taken a financial adviser an hour (and a mountain of paperwork) before persuading a consumer to invest in a savings bond or a pension.[13]

However, moralising now about 'feckless, irresponsible' consumers taking on too much debt, or not saving for a rainy day, adds insult to injury. Many lower income households don't have the option of saving for the future and have no choice to but to borrow to make ends meet or maintain even a semblance of a decent lifestyle in a modern consumer society. Financially excluded households need access to fair, affordable credit to survive.

But access to affordable credit is already a serious problem for the three or four million households with lower incomes or with impaired credit ratings who are not commercially attractive for mainstream lenders and are forced to turn to the 'sub-prime' market or denied access to credit altogether.

Vulnerable households are also disproportionately affected by rising household utility and food bills and will find it even harder to build up a decent cushion in the form of savings to protect themselves against the risks and shocks life throws at them as we enter a more unpredictable, uncertain time for the UK economy. So the challenge of reversing the trends and encouraging lower income households to save rather than borrow is made even more difficult.

However, the credit union model is very suitable for encouraging savings and responsible, sustainable borrowing. The basic model which depends on consumers saving and then borrowing is better at encouraging a culture of thrift and self-help and self-sufficiency.

Moreover, the mutual model which is put into effect by the 'common bond' can encourage a culture of co-operation, shared collective responsibility for and mutual dependency on others. Therefore, there is a strong case for believing that credit unions can help build and maintain communities. In suggesting that credit unions can help build strong communities it should be stressed that the cause and effect can be difficult to disentangle. Looking at the urban areas in Great Britain in which credit unions have been a measurable success, these tend to be areas where strong, identifiable communities already exist. The Irish communities in Glasgow are a case in point as are Caribbean and Nigerian communities in London.

This book offers a Christian perspective on the financial crisis and again it would seem that credit unions do seem to embody Christian principles in practice in financial markets and communities. The idea of operating on a not-for-profit basis, putting mutual benefit before profit, the practice of prudence, putting surplus to good use by making credit available to other members of the community, and shared collective responsibility for others less powerful than ourselves seems to fit in with Christian principles. It is important not to ignore the role of secular movements such as civil rights groups or political parties in helping credit unions and other community-based lenders organise and thrive but, even on a practical level, the churches and influential individual clergy have been hugely influential in helping credit unions thrive in certain communities.

Moreover, it could be argued that the mutual ethos of the credit union movement also fits very well with the views on the financial crisis set out by His Holiness Pope Benedict XVI in his recent Encyclical Letter *Caritas in veritate*. As Pope

Benedict puts it: 'Economic activity cannot solve all social problems through the simple application of commercial logic. This needs to be directed towards the pursuit of the common good, for which the political community in particular must also take responsibility.'[14] Pope Benedict goes on to say that: 'Solidarity is first and foremost a sense of responsibility on the part of everyone with regard to everyone and it cannot therefore be merely delegated to the State.'[15]

So, setting out the limitations of market and state solutions, Pope Benedict explains that: 'Alongside profit-oriented private enterprise and the various types of public enterprise, there must be room for commercial entities based on mutualist principles and pursuing social ends to take root and express themselves. It is from their reciprocal encounter in the marketplace that one may expect hybrid forms of commercial behaviour to emerge, and hence an attentiveness to ways of civilizing the economy'.

This provides a clear economic and moral argument for credit unions if there ever was one.

WHAT MORE NEEDS TO BE DONE?

There are only two ways of providing for financially excluded consumers. The government could force lenders to lend to them by treating banks as utilities like electricity or gas companies. This is an option but the government and regulators could find it difficult to square the circle of forcing the major banks to lend directly to riskier households while at the same time putting lenders under severe pressure to act prudently and restore balance sheets.

The other option is for government to lend directly to the most vulnerable in society and/or to help alternative, not-for-profit (nfp) lenders. Nfp lenders such as credit unions and community development finance institutions (CDFIs) provide an affordable alternative to commercial sub-prime lenders for financially excluded consumers. However, despite the apparent advantages of nfp lenders, as outlined above they have achieved fairly limited penetration[16] compared with the scale achieved by commercial non-prime lenders (such as home credit firms) in Great Britain. Credit unions have reached only a fraction of the number of households that need affordable credit. Commercial non-prime lenders of various types lent at least £4.3 billion in 2005. In comparison, the total lent by nfp lenders (including the Government through the social fund) amounted to around £1 billion.[17]

Commercial non-prime lenders are well entrenched in local communities as a result of their business model (based on door-to-door collections). Nfp lenders cannot compete effectively unless they have access to additional, sustainable resources to compete – on the doorstep.

To be fair to the government, it has improved the position of people facing repossession but the growth in financial exclusion is a much greater systemic problem that needs tackling. Credit unions and other community-based lenders need additional resources if they are to make a significant impact on long-term financial exclusion.

The additional funding could come from three sources. The most obvious is from central and local government. Spending just a tiny fraction of the taxpayers' money used to prop up the major banks by underwriting loans made by nfp lenders would significantly increase the pool of credit for vulnerable communities. The second source is the financial services industry itself. There is a strong moral and economic case for introducing a financial exclusion levy on the banks to make them pay restitution for the damage they have caused to our financial system. At the very least the UK needs its own version of the US Community Reinvestment Act so that banks are forced to become more transparent about the number of households they exclude. The third option is for government to encourage new forms of social investment funds which trades unions, pension funds and ethical investors could use to invest in vulnerable communities through ethically run, nfp lenders.

However, even nfp lenders have their limits. For many of the poorest households the only meaningful option is for government to lend them interest-free money through the social fund.

Overall, there is no shortage of policy options for the government if it wants to protect the most vulnerable in society from the worst of the financial storm.

NOTES

1   http://www.abcul.org/page/about/saving.cfm
2   "Annual Percentage Rate" is the generally accepted measure of the effective rate of interest paid on a loan.
3   Source: Moneyfacts/LendersCompared.org.uk as at end February 2009.
4   Source: Moneysupermarket.com – as at end February 2009.
5   http://www.abcul.org/page/about/people.cfm
6   http://www.abcul.org/page/about/settingup.cfm
7   World Council of Credit Unions (WCCU), Statistical Report, 2007.
8   World Council of Credit Unions (WCCU), Statistical Report, 2007.
9   Penetration here is defined as total number of credit union members as a proportion of the economically active population. Care must be taken with this measure as multiple memberships can artificially increase the penetration rate. For example, on this measure credit unions in Ireland have achieved a penetration rate of 104%!
10 The WCCU reports that Ireland accounted for US$22 billion of total European assets amounting to US$28 billion.
11 http://www.abcul.org/page/statistics.cfm
12 See *Are banks and building societies playing fair?* The Financial Inclusion Centre, www.inclusioncentre.org.uk
13 This is not necessarily an argument for deregulating the sale of pension and investment products.
14 Paragraph 36, chapter three, Fraternity, Economic Development and Civil Society, *Caritas in veritate*.
15 Paragraph 38, chapter three , Fraternity, Economic Development and Civil Society, *Caritas in veritate*.
16 There are some exceptions such as parts of Northern Ireland, Scotland and Merseyside.
17 Credit unions made around £257million in new loans in 2005, while CDFIs increased their lending and investment by around £77 million (only £3m of this was for personal loans). £688 million was provided through The Social Fund in 2006/7.

HARD TIMES AND THE SERVICE OF LOVE: THE FINANCIAL CRASH AND CHARITIES

PHILIPPA GITLIN and DAVID REDFERN

Philippa Gitlin is Director, Caritas SocialActionNetwork.
David Redfern is Charity Fundraising Consultant.

———

INTRODUCTION

In his first encyclical, *Deus caritas est*, published in 2005, Pope Benedict XVI writes 'Love of neighbour, grounded in the love of God, is first and foremost a responsibility for each individual member of the faithful, but it is also a responsibility for the entire ecclesial community at every level: from the local community to the particular Church and to the Church universal in its entirety. As a community, the Church must practise love. Love thus needs to be organised if it is to be an ordered service to the community.'

The Catholic community in the United Kingdom has a long tradition of practising love of neighbour through organised services. Throughout the years, the Church has frequently been the first port of call for those experiencing financial hardship, particularly during economic downturns. Today there are many Catholic charities within England and Wales responding to a wide variety of social care needs of marginalised and vulnerable children, families and older people and this chapter is an attempt to assess the impact of the current economic difficulties on these charities.

Caritas Social Action Network is the umbrella organisation of charities with a Catholic ethos, providing professional social care within England and Wales. Feedback from Caritas member agencies as well as from other Catholic social care charities has provided insight into the impact of the financial crash and subsequent economic difficulties on service delivery as well as on any organisational issues that have developed since September 2008.

As such, this chapter represents an overview of the big issues facing Catholic care organisations and provides suggestions on how to address these challenges. We have no reason to believe that the situation in non-Catholic Christian charities is significantly different.

DEMAND FOR SERVICES

A mixed picture

From the period of September 2008 to the present, demand for services has remained constant for most Caritas member agencies. This may be because, as a comment from Fr Hudson's Society in Birmingham asserts: "Ironically as most of our community projects work mainly with people on benefits they are less affected by unemployment issues", and Nugent Care in Liverpool states that "our new family resettlement service has experienced an increase in referrals which we believe to be due to the fact that the project is new and only just becoming established rather than because of the recession as the problems experienced by the people using the service are long-standing difficulties."

Organisations providing residential care for older people have not noticed significant increase in demand for places, as would be expected, but several commented that where residents' own houses are still waiting to be sold, the lack of fee receipts is causing cash flow pressures.

Problems in adoption and fostering agencies

Adoption and fostering agencies, however, report that local authority budget constraints will have an impact on the support packages available to children and adoptive families. Anecdotal evidence suggests that some local authority social workers are no longer seeking families via voluntary adoption agencies in order to save on the inter-agency fee (the fee paid to the voluntary agency on an adoption placement). This may result in children, particularly those who may have more complex care needs, remaining in care rather than being adopted. One adoption agency reported that three families had 'put on hold' the process of assessment as potential adopters due to economic problems and the impact of redundancy.

Most local authorities have declared that they will not increase the fees they pay to voluntary agencies for children's and for older people's services. Despite this, they are demanding a higher level of service provision (in terms of services covered by the fee) and imposing price review processes to demonstrate 'best value' and 'added value'. This results in additional costs for service providers, as local authorities seek, through this mechanism, to reduce fees paid. All our member agencies commented on the tendency in local authorities to reduce fees and that these reduced fees failed to reflect unavoidable cost increases – especially related to staffing and energy.

Cabrini Children's Society noted that since September 2008, the organisation has experienced an increase in demand for schools' counselling services, nursery places, after school care for children up to eight years, an increase in the number of former children's home residents seeking access to records, and an increase in post adoption referrals. Cabrini has experienced difficulty in meeting these needs because of insufficient funding. Staff also believe that the post adoption needs of families may be being exacerbated by the recession.

Many Catholic charities are facing increased demands

Whilst, as has been mentioned, the demand for services from many Catholic charities has not increased significantly, our research has demonstrated that demands on the services of some agencies has risen. This applies notably to those providing food, clothing, and household goods (such as furniture); those providing housing advice; and those providing advice on debt, employment and migrant rights.

For example, the St Vincent de Paul Society (Chester & Ellesmere Port District Furniture Unit) report that since September 2008, sales (and demands for sales) of furniture and household goods has at times outstripped supply of donated furniture. They state: 'Most of the funding comes from sales of furniture, but we do have some money from the local authority in the form of a grant to assist the re-housing of homeless people. We have not received any grants for this financial year, but this is due (we are informed) to the change of structure in the local authority, and we will eventually be requested to restart our service for the homeless.'

St Vincent's Furniture Store Sheffield, reports that due to the economic downturn, with people losing their jobs and even their homes, there has been a 35% increase in demand for their service of recycled furniture which is supplied to the homeless and other vulnerable people in Sheffield. They are the only organisation in the city that can offer immediate relief, free of charge, in helping people out of homelessness.

St Cuthbert's Care in Newcastle-upon-Tyne launched the 'Clothing Bus' in October 2008 as a clothing service which provides donated clothes to those in need. The bus visits poor communities distributing clothes for a nominal amount of 5p. An average of 1,800 people per month access the service. Those running the service have witnessed first hand the destitute lives of families who simply do not have enough to live on. A spokesperson for St Cuthbert's Care states 'As it is a relatively new initiative we do not have evidence to state that the success of this service is directly related to the recession. However we do believe that given the economic climate it was a very timely initiative. Furthermore we have recently opened a '5p' shop in Sunderland where there is a high rate of unemployment. This has been equally successful. We hope in the future to purchase another bus which will serve more outlying communities in the areas where there is deprivation.'

The Passage, a day centre for homeless adults in Victoria, London, has noted more of their service users saying they became homeless as a result of losing their jobs. Staff at The Passage also report an increase in migrants from the new EU accession countries being entrenched in street homelessness as a consequence of unemployment.

In February 2009, Cardinal Hume Centre in London conducted its third Survey of Client Need, which reflects the 'real concerns and aspirations of the Centre's clients as well as evidence of the realities of life in England in 2009.'[1]

Through the survey, the following issues were highlighted:

- Household income – 66% of the interviewees were living below the official recognised poverty line and 26% had at least one child in the household.

- At the time, 75% of people were concerned about the recession. Since then, a financial advice centre has been opened which has seen a big demand. At present funding allows for an advisor one day a week who sees four clients a day.

- 24% of clients stated that they had one or more children in their household although only 19% said they were claiming child tax credit. Cardinal Hume's financial advice service is providing much needed advice on benefit entitlements to those who would otherwise be unaware of them.

- 59% of those surveyed said they were experiencing problems obtaining employment, or barriers to employment such as: child care costs; language barriers or barriers caused by immigration status; having a criminal record; and age discrimination. All of these clients asked if the Centre would be able to help them to overcome the barriers.

- The majority of clients were not UK citizens (just 49%). An immigration advisory service was introduced due to heavy demand in November 2008. Since then, the Advisor has seen 132 people for immigration advice.

- Just under half of those interviewed had no fixed address, with the majority living in hostels and 16% living in private rented accommodation. 1% were sleeping on the street. Only 20% were in council accommodation. Those in private rented accommodation had trouble collecting enough for a deposit for a landlord (for example, the first month's rent) and Cardinal Hume Centre receives a lot of requests for help with this.

Housing Justice, the umbrella organisation for charities providing accommodation and housing advice, reported that many people living in private rented accommodation are becoming homeless as a result of their landlords losing properties due to economic difficulties – an indirect consequence which perhaps many people would not have anticipated. Many of these homeless families are undocumented migrants but who have roots in the community (for example, children attending local schools, or parents working). Night shelters across the country report more people from EU accession countries seeking accommodation, with women being in the majority.

Caritas Social Action Network's member organisations report concern over staff retention since the onset of the recession. Organisations have noted over the last year an increasing number of applications for employment state 'made redundant due to company/business closure' and people are applying for jobs as carers who have never previously worked in the care sector.

Many projects have insufficient funding to retain full staffing complements and inevitably staff redundancies follow reductions in funding. Difficulties in supplementing any shortfall in fees paid by local authorities for any of our agencies' services are made worse because of a marked decrease in voluntary income and investment income due to the recession.

FUNDRAISING TO FINANCE SERVICES

The general picture

Depending on the work of the charity, funding comes from an ever-widening range of sources. Since 2000, government funding has played an increasingly important role for many charities, with some being almost exclusively funded through service-level agreements and contracts. Some of these run over several years but many are limited to just one year. The role of the voluntary sector in delivering social services in our communities was emphasised by the creation of the government's 'Office of the Third Sector' in May 2006. It was set up in recognition of the increasingly important role that voluntary organisations play in the community. We will look at the impact this may have a little later.

However, traditionally, charities have sought to raise funds to carry out their purpose from many other sources. These include the general public, charitable trusts, fundraising events, companies, legacies, trading and sponsorship. Charities have employed a range of fundraisers to carry out the job of securing the necessary funds.

In any financial model, an organisation looks to spread the risk of its sources of funds, the most vulnerable being those reliant on one major customer. For charities it is a similar picture. Charities or other non-profit organisations setting up programmes exclusively funded by either a single contract or donation do need to have a plan in place for what happens at the end of that funding period.

In terms of how the credit crunch has affected charities, there is a mixed picture. There have been some high profile losses that have led to redundancies and a cut back in the services provided. On the other hand, many charities are working their way through the financial turmoil, apparently facing very little impact.

At one end of the scale organisations such as the National Society for the Prevention of Cruelty to Children (NSPCC) and British Red Cross reported deep concerns towards the end of 2008 and the start of 2009. Both are examples of charities with highly sophisticated fundraising systems which rely on donations from the public and from the corporate sector. These are the very two areas that appear to be most affected in the short term. A survey of 362 charities by PWC, the Institute of Fundraising and the Charity Finance Directors' Group reveals that charity incomes are expected to fall in real terms and costs to rise. PWC estimates that the shortfall could reach £2.3bn in 2009.

However in the most recent survey of charity chief executives there is an increasing feeling of optimism. A growing number of charity leaders believe that recovery will be over the next 12 months and 'things' will get back to 'normal'.[2]

The extent of the impact of the credit crunch does, in part, seem to depend on the way charities are funded. However, it also depends on the charitable cause. For the largest charities that rely on huge numbers of individual donations, adding up to tens of millions of pounds a year, together with corporate donations, even a relatively small decline in giving can mean a cut of services and staff. Any recovery in corporate giving will probably require a recovery in corporate profits. If companies are making a loss, little or no funding will find its way into charitable giving.

Legacies

Another invaluable source of funding for many charities, especially those that have been established for some time, is legacies. It is quite logical to assume that legacy income will be reduced. Firstly the property market has dropped and the sale price of a property is an important part of many legacies. Secondly interest rates have dropped dramatically. Many people have been reliant on interest on savings as a source of income. If interest rates remain low for some time, the only option for many will be to use their capital to sustain their standard of living. Over time this will erode the value of estates that are left to charities as legacies.

There is a third threat to legacy income. With the financial situation uncertain and with the prospect of large Inheritance Tax being due on death, many who had planned to leave a legacy may choose to support their own families whilst they are living, especially if one of their children or a niece or nephew is in need. In this way they will see the value of their legacy whilst they are living.

Donations from trusts

A huge source of income to many charities, especially those delivering frontline services, is Charitable Trust income. The top twenty-five Trusts alone gave £958.9million in 2007/8. This has increased dramatically over the past fifteen years by about 290%[3]. This money goes to fund the truly voluntary work of the third sector, funding everything from staffing to equipment, buildings to holidays for those in need.

There are several possible major threats to this income. Many of the top trusts were set up with an endowment, a lump sum of money or shares, and their giving is from the interest earned on that endowment in the previous year. Income from dividends and interest will have fallen – in many cases significantly. Where giving is from capital, capital values of trusts' investments will also have fallen substantially in the last two years – though, at the time of writing, share prices are rising again. Whilst the amount of money available from trusts decreases, the need for the work carried out by the charities increases. Trusts have reported a greater call on their income and have received a substantial increase in the number of applications.

There is a longer term threat that is linked to the development of many services funded by central government, local authorities or one of the many other statutory agencies. Charitable Trusts and Foundations are generally very clear that they will not fund activities that are a statutory responsibility. Examples would be housing vulnerable people, children's services and many forms of education. If the funding from government for these activities currently carried out by charities were to be reduced or cut, then charitable trusts are highly unlikely to step in to fund any rescue package, in fact many are legally unable to do so because of their constitutions.

This brings us back to the issue of statutory funding and how stable that will be in the near future. The government, in some form or other, is the single largest funder of the voluntary sector. According to the National Council for Voluntary Organisations (NCVO) £12billion of the charity sector's £33billion yearly income comes from statutory sources. Government tax receipts are falling and, therefore, keeping support of the sector at its current level would mean increased government borrowing, spending reserves or reducing other budgets. The likelihood must be that funds will be harder to come by and some services could be cut or reduced.

Voluntary funding

Almost at the other end of the spectrum of charity fundraising is the charity shop. Run by an army of volunteers and ranging widely in sophistication, they raise invaluable funds every day. They are likely to be busier in a time of economic difficulties than ever. More and more people go into charity shops looking for essentials or a bargain. Increased demand needs an increased supply of goods to sell. However there is some evidence that the supply is dropping off. One charity that runs a number of furniture and clothes stores, reports a problem of maintaining a supply of good quality second-hand goods: especially items such as sofas. People are buying new items less often so the charity shop misses out on the second-hand donation. A second change has been that with websites such as *eBay*, it is now easier than ever to sell unwanted goods and make a bit of money to go towards a new purchase.

Most of us come closest to charities through their appeals for funds. This includes everything from Christian Aid week, appeals after Mass or other Christian services, adverts in the press, TV campaigns, celebrity endorsed appeals, mail through the door, fundraisers on the streets, and telephone calls. If it touches us we respond. This side of fundraising relies on the general public having either spare cash or being prepared to give sacrificially.

Following a recent appeal by a charity, a lady wrote back:

"Dear Sirs, I have supported your charity for the past ten years and I hope that in my own small way my contribution has been able to help the young people in your care. However I regret to say that the enclosed donation will be my last. My nephew was recently made redundant and whilst he has managed to find another job it is not as well paid. He has a wife and two teenage girls and I have decided to help him out with his mortgage payments."

You can understand that lady's actions, and I am sure her nephew is himself a most worthy beneficiary of her money. This lady may, by her actions, have prevented a far greater cost to society – and possibly to charities – by helping her nephew stay in his house.

It is clear that public appeals have struggled, especially for the larger charities that are reliant on this form of fundraising for millions of pounds. This has resulted in services being cut and some redundancies in the sector.

But all is not doom and gloom. There are clear examples of charities, especially faith-based charities, still generating enough funding to keep services running and even to expand in many areas. Perhaps it is worth thinking about the relationships between the donors and the charities to understand why this occurs. The closer the empathy of the donor to the organisation, the more likely the donor will be to continue their support, looking to save money in other areas. This is where many of the smaller charities have a big advantage over larger well-known charities. They are very unlikely to have a marketing department, in fact letters asking for funding may well be initiated by the manager or chief executive, and donors who respond are likely to have a long-term association with the charity. They feel they know where the money will go and there is a greater level of trust. They may also be acutely aware of the difficulties the charity may be facing.

There is also another factor affecting the different impact on charities in this current crisis. In business, the years of plenty were accompanied by big bonuses. There was little saving for a rainy day, let alone a full-blown storm. Charities on the other hand have been significantly more prudent during the prosperous years. Their governance models have helped maintain pay levels, even at the very top, and the payment of bonuses has long been resisted by the sector. Charities have also been encouraged to build sufficient reserves 'just in case'. Those who have done this carefully are well set to weather the storm and replenish their reserves when funds are more readily available.

CONCLUSION: THE 'OPTION FOR THE POOR' IS NOT A DISCRETIONARY ACTIVITY

In the current hard times it is worth reminding ourselves that the 'option for the poor' is one of the basic principles of Catholic social teaching, which asserts that the deprivation and powerlessness of the poor wounds the whole community, and that the moral test of a society is how it treats its most vulnerable members. In his latest encyclical, *Caritas in veritate*, published in 2009, Pope Benedict XVI says 'The more we strive to secure a common good corresponding to the real needs of our neighbours, the more effectively we love them. Every Christian is called to practise this charity, in a manner corresponding to his vocation and according to the degree of influence he wields in the *pólis*.'

The Christian voluntary sector is underpinned by its belief that the option for the poor is an essential part of society's effort to achieve the common good, and that a healthy community can be achieved only if its members give special attention to those with special needs, to those who are poor and on the margins of society. For centuries therefore Christian charities in the UK have worked hard to sustain the support they give to the marginalised and vulnerable in our society. Undoubtedly the faith-based voluntary sector will strive throughout the current hard times with the same determination to ensure that continues to meet the needs of people affected by the current economic crisis.

NOTES

1   Cardinal Hume Centre 2009 Survey, entitled 'Are we listening?'
2   As reported in the NCVO report of 24 June 2009
3   Reported in *Directory of Social Change – A guide to major Trusts 2007/8.*

SOCIAL INNOVATION AND HABITS OF THE HEART: RE-INVENTING CHRISTIAN MISSION IN THE FACE OF RECESSION

FRANCIS DAVIS

Francis Davis is Director of the Las Casas Institute on Ethics, Governance and Social Responsibility at Blackfriars Hall, Oxford and a Visiting Fellow at the Helen Suzman Foundation in Johannesburg. He was previously a founder board member and Chair of the SCA Group, one of the UK's leading social enterprises.

———

In this chapter I want to risk some minefields of possible miscommunication and misunderstanding to make a tentative proposal. I would like to suggest that the current economic crisis calls for a new theory, inventiveness and strategy of mission on the part of British Christian institutions[1] in general, and a fresh focus for the churches' educational bodies in particular.

My proposal is tentative in that it represents reflection on a "work in progress". It draws on ongoing interviews and surveys of hundreds of senior staff in "Christian organisations" as to their understanding of "leadership", "mission", "service", "justice" and "impact" today.[2] It also builds on ongoing aspects of the research and public debate engendered by my 2008 publication, *Moral – But No Compass*.[3] That report found its way onto the front page of *The Times*, national public radio in the US, was praised by the conservative press in their leader columns, attacked by liberal commentators and the subject of a series of parliamentary debates. The Conservative front bench called it "formidable", and Archbishops of Canterbury and York "fascinating and important".

At the outset I wish to acknowledge certain limitations arising from my academic location on an island in secularising Western Europe.[4] In the UK and in Ireland discussion of the form of church-state relations are *au courant* and intertwined with debate as to the nature of "secularisation" and the role of state funding of "religious" bodies. I have argued elsewhere that these are complex and new waters for churches to navigate.[5] Indeed the whole matter is further complicated in the UK by the comparatively underdeveloped state of the social scientific study of explicitly – and vaguely – Christian organisations.

Nevertheless it is my hope that a kernel of the argument will be transferable for those working in a variety of UK regions – and especially for those whose institutions face situations of intense social exclusion and poverty. For in these times of economic hardship and social insecurity the churches have a special duty to reach out to those most at risk.

First, I will turn to what I judge to be some important questions for institutional leadership in Christian institutions. Next, I will argue in favour of a redevelopment of a tradition of a common search for truth through deliberate disputation. In doing so I will suggest that Christian institutions may discover a more profound rootedness in emerging trends in the social sciences and management studies than some forms of theology have allowed us in changing times. With this in mind I will argue, lastly, that the Christian churches are now at a unique juncture, with an unprecedented opportunity to launch new institutions, to renew the public sphere and serve the neediest. That is to say they have a niche contribution to make in the face of the economic crisis.

LEADERSHIP, LANGUAGE AND CHURCH

It can be dangerous for a social scientist with an interest in management and leadership to contribute to a work that also includes contributions from eminent theologians. For theologians of hope, social research findings can seem reductive – or (with reason) to have passed into the realms of spurious "scientific" claim. They can stand accused of losing all the spirit of poetry that those in search of the spirit and grace celebrate.[6] For church historians current practical questions of governance often seem trivial when benchmarked against the tides and challenges of time. For those from many other backgrounds the very introduction of "management" discourse into the realm of "mission" represents a form of treachery by risking, it could be suggested, the "commodification" of a theological process whose focus should be the ultimate destination of human flourishing.[7]

Others may respond with the much less nuanced allegation that high principles are delightful and desirable but funds are scarce, the external environment constantly changing and the institutional pressures enormous. Especially in an environment where we have been promised public sector retrenchment (and can expect private and third sector restructuring) they long for church leaders and activists to "get real".

Consequently, in setting out to discuss the current contribution, and future potential, of mission in and from UK Christian churches and especially what they may contribute at a time of social risk, we need to pay particular attention to language, the potential for inter-disciplinary miscommunication, and the need to persist in a common search for truth. "Community" is a word which is often used in Christian and charitable mission statements[8] – and yet it can hide an inward looking culture, glacial governance procedures and a huge resistance to the very change that real conversion demands.[9] Often it also acts as cover to a profound disagreement as to the nature and purpose of faith itself. Likewise "Gospel values" which, when examined more closely, may turn out to be an equal opportunities statement much thinner in philosophical intent than even the claims to a normative justice made by some secular political parties.[10]

Worse still, it is conceivable that terms which may have had a common meaning in cultures of Christianity gone by (or in one global region) may be unravelling in the face of secularisation or the pressures of the "accountingisation" of society that (arguably) characterise the modern age.[11] Even a term such as "preaching" may be contested: one outlook on Christian life may suggest that "preaching" is undertaken only by an ordained person at the Eucharistic service while others maintain it is valuable only if linked to numerical performance criteria of "converts brought home". Others still may view preaching as a task of all of the baptised as they engage in communicative activities that contribute to the rebuilding of a public sphere which has been hollowed out by the privatisation of discourse, principles and behaviour – including the search for sanctity itself.[12]

Confusion over terms can mean that in practice a Christian institution and the behaviours of those linked to it have become identical to any other, except for some of the language it uses about itself. At the other extreme staff teams and stakeholders can feel radically disempowered because of the enormousness of the brief they have been handed – for example, to "prepare students for death" or "seek radical structural social renewal".[13] In between those points, when told the institution stands for "kingdom values" they look about blankly – but without daring to admit – that they are wondering how to turn such an expression into practice that afternoon.[14]

A serious approach to language is then vital for strategic missionary reasons. Inside the metaphors of theology may be built a tendency to an "ought" by which we might seek to order the institution but which distracts us, no matter how unintentionally, from the "is" of the practical challenges we face and the particular local conversations we need to pursue, especially in a recession. How are we to align "community", "vision", "inspiration", "mission" "resources" and "impact" if the words have multiple meanings?

Such deliberate reflection is particularly important in secular settings: "spirituality", "faiths", "faith motivation", "justice" and "common good" are all words used by church leaders and Cabinet ministers when they meet, but do they share a vocabulary and a grammar? In order to attempt to link theory, practice and delivery so that principles become not personal "beliefs"- the classical secularist close-down on the wonder of a full faith – *ways of life*, rich habits of virtue expressed through organisations as well as persons are needed.[15]

In this environment every kind of Christian institution becomes a work of *applied* theology – a hard headed daily pilgrimage to authenticity between an unconditionally marketised "product" and an admirable (but fearful) "purity".[16] This pilgrimage is carried out in the context of churches which can be increasingly polarised and in societies which are almost certainly increasingly so.[17]

The ground of knowledge formation in the Christian churches then needs to be an open enthusiasm for debate involving all sides of a conversation. By this I do not suggest a simple lurch to "free speech" (important though that may be) but that a central feature of the formation of the congregational, diocesan, circuit – or online – resources of the Christian community should be a robust encouragement to a rich *disputation* that opens (and holds together) fresh spaces for argument.

Common meanings, common terms and common vision are much more likely to emerge from a common life than from a fractious individualism or communitarian partisanship, Christian churches need to model such a struggle towards a common culture – or community of character – to both the wider church and society for, as we shall see in the next section, they are increasingly under threat.

Ironically it is the new waves of management studies, and the wider social sciences, which many Christians have treated with such suspicion, in which there are emerging patterns which might assist.[18]

A CHURCH THAT KNOWS ITS PLACE: CONTEXT AND ANALYSIS

Among other activities, in 2008-09 my colleagues and I undertook two major pieces of research: the first, for the Church of England, I have already mentioned. It concentrated on the Anglican contribution to social welfare. The second study sought to quantify the scale of the English Catholic community's work alongside migrants, asylum seekers and refugees.

It was striking for us that at the outset many Anglican Bishops reported that the Church of England's contribution "had declined" or "was no longer significant" and how this was a source of "sadness" for them. In fact, in the sphere of social welfare and voluntary action we found the opposite to be the case.[19]

137

In contrast, the Catholic Bishops had invested a good deal of energy in expressing publicly their solidarity with "the stranger" and yet we found that Catholic action in the refugee field was more patchy than might have been expected: for example, the diocese of one senior bishop was a peak area of asylum seeker dispersal, and yet there has been *no* response at all from the local Church despite media comment from the Ordinary concerned.[20]

Perhaps more controversially the formal Catholic position on relationships and sexuality are well known. Nevertheless, in a further survey of 1,000 Mass-going Catholics we found upwards of 80% of those interviewed had life practices at variance with the Church's teaching. A majority expressed disagreement with the formal position (even when they did not know what it was!).[21]

Meanwhile, CAFOD and Georgetown University have recently published research that when combined shows that official estimates of how many Catholics there are in England and Wales are understated to the tune of a million. Conversely, the number of Mass going Catholics is overstated by 100,000.

In short, and it may seem trite to re-state it, churches, in fragmenting cultures – or societies under pressure – may share a written "vision", or even a self description, which is out of kilter with the social reality within and around them.

This can be addressed partly by the disputation that I have referred to above. Additionally I want to suggest that in truly discerning our place in local neighbourhoods, national polities and global societies, even Christian institutions that would seek to emphasise their orientation, or disciplinary priority, as "theological"[22] need to turn to empirical research. In the 2008 study referred to above, my colleagues and I established that the UK state had no idea of – nor intention of evidencing – the faith-based contribution to civic welfare despite claiming a coherent "faith and social cohesion strategy" by which to guide all government departments, and the allocation of financial resources[23]. The churches had not even noticed some of the key patterns we uncovered.[24]

In a climate of "evidence-based policy making"[25] our discovery of the lack of research in faith-based areas revealed the conversation between the state and Christian institutions to be grounded in policy-making sand. Conversely, the other research referred to above suggests that sometimes "outsiders" know more about us than we (or at least some Christian leaders) dare admit to ourselves.

More crucially still, if the churches could not provide – or value – evidence about themselves then might this not also suggest that their own planning for mission could be as unrooted as the state's policy judgments? Political witness, for example, would consequently be at risk of being muddled despite exhortation towards "social teaching", "political theology" – or even generous secondments of staff to ecclesiastical commissions to draft innumerable statements on the "ethics of society".[26]

While we renew our conversations about leading the churches then we also need to renew the means by which we discern the patterns of the "places" and networks that we serve.

In doing so we might inspire the Christian community as well by enabling it to see more clearly what it *could* do because it is now clear what it is not *actually* doing: the local church may want to focus its resources on "the youth, the unchurched and the homeless",[27] despite the demographic directions flowing around it which suggest it should focus on the migrant, the old and the long-term unemployed – or never employed. Nudging the church back to social reality is an eminently "useful" role for a Christian church and its leadership as they clarify their own duties and plans at a time of social crisis.

In preparing such clarifications we may, if my interviewees are to be believed, discover that because of an over-dependency on state funds in some quarters, an inflexible state structure in others, a destroyed civic sphere, or extreme consumerism, no longer assume notions of a rich "common good" as a starting point for our efforts. Instead we may have to turn to the potential for the Christian community and its institutions

– to become places of relevant institutional renewal in the new dark ages which are upon us.[28]

It is to these questions that I now turn.

IDEAS, INSTITUTIONS AND THE PUBLIC REALM

Sophisticated assessments of the rise of the New Right as a force to convert minds, hearts and cultures in the last century repeatedly note the profound seriousness with which that movement took organisations and institutions as vehicles and locations to embed civic outlooks, cultural aspirations and policy habits.[29] Dionne even suggests that in the case of US neo-conservatives such a concern with right thinking about ideas and institutions arose from lessons learnt by neo-conservatives during youthful sallies into the "New Left".[30]

Consequently, in a reversal of the New Left allegation that elite forces in society set out to capture the state for their own purposes[31] the cultural New Right sought to take control of school boards, state-level bodies and certain private and charitable entities. Rather as Friars invented the new institutional form of the mendicant preaching order to reach unchurched urban centres, so also did the conservative Right invent its own new institutions to carry its principles, habits and vision into the public square.

New right think tanks have been among the most entrepreneurial entities on the planet, have worked together to support common goals and continue to reach out with an astounding focus. They share a commitment to the development of recognisable and "high quality" brands and they identify clear "arenas" or "publics" with whom they wish to communicate. They also develop a deep knowledge of the patterns of life – and decision making – of those within these "arenas". Although they have a "clear line" such think tanks are explicitly independent developing particular gifts of transcending traditional boundaries between the private, public and voluntary sectors in order to maximise their personal networks and institutional impact on cultures.

To assist in all of this the neo-conservative movements also gathered around them new philanthropic resources. This included some foundations specifically focused on backing those who seek to launch fresh institutions in Eastern Europe and Asia especially.[32]

In Rome, for example, the Acton Institute has set itself the task of educating young seminarians at Santa Croce and Gregorian universities to name but two, while at Washington DC's Heritage Foundation "network co-ordinators" support ideological allies across the country, and match new donors with intellectual entrepreneurs wanting to establish fresh conservative think tanks.[33] Their approaches to dissemination, and highly targeted publication of research findings, can move public and private policy and culture at speed. It is an approach now being emulated by a new wave of "think" and "do" tanks on the moderate UK left[34] and thus no wonder that Giddens has argued that, at least until the ongoing liquidity crisis for banks, neo-liberalism was the only "revolutionary" ideology on the planet.[35]

The successes of the New Right are significant for reflection on Christian mission because they locate ideas distribution in very specific settings (despite much normative core content) and link them to new "legs" by which to journey, namely niche networks within the full range of dominant institutions between and within state, business and civil society.

In the Christian setting certain denominations may sometimes be at risk of giving inadequate attention to such institutional variation and focus: especially in Episcopal denominations huge claims can be made about the potential of a "congregation" (as the local expression of a wider theological reality) but when they begin new ventures this actually causes the congregation to start out with an innate sense of powerlessness. [36]Vision is not matched to the capacity of institutional vehicles – but is then still called "prophecy".

In turn this may hinder potential to distribute ideas – our words – and the embedding of habits that might arise from them. Dreams become unlinked from the means to sustain them or fall back on existing structures while still claiming "newness". Alternatively "statements" or "resolutions" are released without a clear understanding of the "publics" to be addressed.[37]

For example, an established church (and ours has) may seek out "fresh expressions" of mission[38] which, despite much fanfare to the contrary, mirror very closely the current geographical forms of work which have emerged in response to previous patterns of social and pastoral need. Likewise, in terrains where a denomination has seen itself as a "national" (albeit not established) church the Christian reflex may be to sustain "the old" at great cost to that which is emerging; rather like a monopoly objecting to incursions from innovative small businesses. The authentic alternative is not, however, to suggest an unreflective escape but to find new ways to start again.

My contention is that the contexts in which the churches find themselves are constantly changing and thus it is unlikely that new wine will fit snugly into old wineskins or grooves. Moreover, as institutional pressures arise on the churches, Christian institutions in particular can become the locus of unbalanced lament or the depository of all of the hopes of church leaderships as they struggle to make sense of new, tough, missionary terrain.[39]

As hopes multiply innumerable images of the church go with them. When those discourses run back into Christian institutions the potential, as I have suggested, for strategic drift leaps as metaphor is piled upon metaphor to defend an ever more inclusive brief.

In seeking to reground our common mission then we need not only to fashion common disputation and root those debates in new social research about the church and society of today. Like the New Right we also need common and compelling institutions and practical projects which mark out our mission niches and demonstrate our zeal. Our new talk and fresh research could then be the basis of renewal and re-invention. It could be the basis of energetic ideas, institutions and impacts as strategic as the New Right but with a much deeper hope on offer for dark ages in which new lights must shine.

CHRISTIAN INSTITUTIONS AS SOCIAL "SILICON VALLEYS"

St John's College with Cranmer Hall, in the University of Durham[40] can lay claim (with justice) to being the founding home of the UK Fairtrade Movement: From within its walls emerged *Tearcraft* which subsequently divided to give birth to Traidcraft which in turn has grown to become the closest thing to an ecumenical UK household "name". At around the same time the college was educating others who would go on to make outstanding national contributions in the field of social entrepreneurship.[41]

Theologically such an interlocking set of developments could be ascribed to the outpouring of grace, or the gifts of the Spirit, but this may run the risk I have touched upon of failing to recognise attributes of Christian *institutions* which enable them to renew their ability to praise, to bless and to preach: while in Durham the Fairtrade cause was being launched, in other parts of the UK the anti-homelessness movement was growing out of Christian-led responses to social need. It culminated in the vital Christian contribution to the first ever British legislation to protect vulnerable homeless people.[42] Since then the Jubilee Debt campaign emerged out of a Christian seminar at Keele University while the Make Poverty History campaign has been nurtured by faith groups. Even the "secular" Amnesty International has its origins in liberal Christianity and continues to be assessed by some as a form of "religionless" faith.[43]

What has changed since those pioneering days is that on the one hand we have learned a good deal about the effects of "clustering" on the potential success of new enterprises while on the other a more structured movement for "social innovation" has emerged on the global stage.[44] It is in relation to this realm of enquiry and action that I want to suggest that the crying need for new institutions by which to embed habits of the heart may be pursued. Christian dioceses, cathedrals, circuits and institutions are well placed to make a distinctive contribution to this especially now that need is increasing and likely to do so more.

"Social innovation" refers to new strategies, concepts, ideas and organisations that meet social and spiritual needs of all kinds – from working conditions and education to community development and health. They also extend and strengthen civil society and assist in the reduction of poverty.

Social innovation can take place within and between each of the public, private and voluntary sectors and can sometimes be seen as a process (for example, open source technologies) or as a way of addressing a social problem (for example, microfinance).

As such, this is not a simplistic call for just another "fresh expression". Nor is it a lament for the lack of an MBA programme with a bit more "sustainability" in its non-profit track. Neither is it just an exhortation to become a more Christian business school because we talk a lot about the virtues or corporate social responsibility. Perhaps even more crucially it is not an advocacy for a traditional extension of community service, mission outreach or community development.

Important though all of those strategies are my argument is that we have not sought to reflect adequately on sources of *Christian* social innovation. In Christian institutions this has robbed us of the opportunity to develop as many common projects as might have been the case.[45] In society it has reduced recognition both of what we contribute and the scale by which we could make a difference in the future.[46]

In, and alongside, Christian institutions (and especially our schools) there are now opportunities to develop physical and virtual Christian social innovation parks – or what I have called elsewhere "social silicon valleys".[47] These would be "hubs" around which the renewal of spiritual zeal and social and civic renewal can be grounded in the tough times ahead.

Social silicon valleys would go further than more utilitarian models that surround us. Firstly, there would be much more systematic learning about how to support social innovation from a faith base and this would build on increasingly sophisticated understandings of social entrepreneurship, enterprise and the impact of mission innovation. Secondly, social silicon valleys would seek to proliferate better ways to spot, create, incubate and scale up good ideas, people and methods so that they can be embedded in existing, new and – crucially – scaleable institutions. Thirdly, Christian communities and bodies would seek to garner new sources (and methods) of support to make such a potential deliverable.

Some will only be able to imagine what such a strategy would look like if I offer concrete examples. So, what might set our social silicon valleys apart?

They would be led by those with direct access to senior church leaders and leading lay Christians. Such a positioning would locate the mission of the social silicon valley at the heart of the Church and across all its activities.[48] I will return to this matter below.

Secondly, they would see themselves as effervescing centres of Christian creativity and would look to attract energetic and mission-centred Christians to them from across the region – and the planet. By this I do not mean the creation of what might be termed an "educational gated community" such as Ave Maria University in Florida, but a new "mission cluster" grounded in gift relationships.

This is not to minimise the insights of spirituality. However, our social silicon valleys would be looking to launch new modes of mission that can be internationalised or adopted by others for roll out on a larger scale. Such things may indeed happen "informally" or "by the grace of God" in many local places but the social silicon valley would structure them, back them and replicate them. It would help them to bypass some of the institutional nightmares that have been common even to clearly holy causes.[49] It would introduce them to the global Christian – and/or faith – community (and beyond).

Moreover, social silicon valleys would have a particular brief to contribute to the renewal of market relationships and voluntary and public sector innovation in these trying times. Despite condemnations in some "rational" economic quarters there is still scope to bring together principle-driven family entrepreneurs, firms from the "Mutual top 300", and unique business forms such as Focolare's "*Economy of Communion*" in shared physical – and virtual – spaces and so to broaden the range of market forms on offer. Indeed, there they could develop new institutions and learn from the best social entrepreneurs in the world. First target for the evidence gathering – to support an open source faith-based international social innovation network – would be the most successful models of practice developed by the faith communities globally in response to community economic hardship. After all, the Christian Church runs more educational and social welfare institutions than it does parishes![50]

As new horizons are broken open, fresh forms of funding to pump prime, and help scale, the social silicon valley's contribution would be needed. While some resources may flow from traditional Christian – or multi-faith – groups, giving a new pooling of effort would give social silicon valleys a regional network, national links and international sources of funds.

These might include the younger generation of faith-based high-net-worth individuals and family foundation members. They are (very often) exasperated by the lack of innovation shown by church leaderships – not to mention the obsession with fixed assets in some dioceses and Christian universities! These young risk takers would be particularly attracted because it would be demonstrating their community at the front end of the innovation curve rather than playing "catch up".[51] Either way, a skill of the institution would be to devise new packages of funding across the public, private, church and philanthropic sectors to develop the social silicon valley's work and contribution as it grew.

Aside from the financial revenues, and perhaps of most interest for those who lead Christian bodies, there is here an institutional opportunity. This new "mission centre" at the heart of core business (or surrounding a large school) would be a strategic means by which to legitimise cross-disciplinary collaboration, community and outreach like never before. This is why it needs to be led with direct "cover" from senior management teams, and by staff and volunteers content to live with uncertainty and between topic areas. The aim is not only to launch (very traditionally) new businesses but to create a mixed economy of private, public, religious, social (and mission) innovations which are intermeshed and mutually supportive.

Very concretely then, a social silicon valley located in, or launched from, a Christian institution should not simply debate the demise of "the faith", the collapse of "finance" or the "decline of virtue" in silos. It would seek less to take on the woes of the whole Christian church and her mission and more to be a locus of institutional renewal of both the Christian church and society. In essence it would become a social and religious research and development centre that enables us to scatter networked, innovative, prophetic institutional fragments across a culture and economy that needs renewal. These institutions will not be new national churches with territorial claims but they will be "communities of character" witnessing to a rich and flourishing humanity and directly addressing social need.

To make concrete such "communities of character" even more they could look like, for example, a Zweite Sparkasse, a Cristo Rey/Studio School, a National Leadership Roundtable on Church Management or the Economy of Communion.

Zweite Sparkasse[52]

Die Zweite Sparkasse was launched in 2006 in a partnership between Erste Bank in Vienna and Caritas Austria. It is a "bank for the unbankable" and spread quickly to Austria's regions. It is staffed wholly by volunteers from the banking sector who gain client referrals because the churches' roots to local neighbourhoods and communities facing poverty are so strong. This experience could be repeated in, for example, the UK where in urban priority areas clergy are often the only "professionals" that actually live locally and where so many local churches have become outlets for the national Post Office.

Services offered by this new social bank include a basic account, a bank card, an investment account with interest and an optional building loan contract. In co-operation with a local insurance provider, cover is also available at a discounted cost. New customers are automatically able to access free legal

147

advice on a quarterly basis. Crucially, the credit account is not a stand-alone product aimed at people in personal distress but forms part of a multi-faceted package of counselling and support services provided by welfare organisations and the churches. In the UK such support might prove timely as incapacity benefit is reined in and unemployment increases dramatically.

Fascinatingly, the model is now being extended to Romania where pyramid selling scandals had damaged the banks even before the current crisis. Here, in rural areas, the Erste Foundation is testing the use of mobile phone technology as a replacement for an excessively costly branch structure. This mirrors the use, in Ireland, of "pay as you go" cards to help African migrants send remittances home to their families.[53]

Cristo Rey/Studio Schools[54]

Cristo Rey schools originated in US inner city areas as a response to the cost of a faith-based education in a setting where the state will not fund church schools and also as a means to combat teenage truancy.

Students attend on four days a week for vocational classes grounded in a strong Christian ethos and on the fifth day – still part of their school week – they do a real job in a real company which has committed to be a "corporate partner".

The vocational skills are meaningful to the students while the "real job" gives them references and social networks from organisations and addresses outside their stereotyped neighbourhoods. Moreover, the students' experience is not simply voluntary work experience – they are in proper part-time employment. The pay they receive makes their education 65% self funding and the sense of responsibility this conveys has slashed truancy rates.

When the UK government heard about *Cristo Rey* Schools they copied it directly including the possibility of developing "*Studio Schools*" in a new education act.

National Leadership Roundtable on Church Management

To quote its mission staement, the National Leadership Roundtable on Church Management (NLRCM) exists as an organisation of laity, religious and clergy working together to promote excellence and best practice in the management, finances and human resources development of the Catholic Church in the USA. It does this by greater incorporation of the expertise of the laity.

Founded in 2005 it was in part a response to the child abuse crisis in US Catholicism but also symbolic of a frustration in some philanthropic circles with the quality of governance in Catholic institutions. Most recently, for example, the NLRCM arranged for the secondment of skilled lay people to assist the Catholic Church and its welfare societies after Hurricane Katrina ravaged southern states.

What is especially interesting today is that the NLRCM is now co-located with the Catholic chaplaincy at Yale University.

Economy of Communion

Inspired by Chiara Lubich, Economy of Communion (EOC) seeks to insert into the marketplace a more "human dimension". EOC businesses work in networks or come together in their own business parks. They commit to sharing a tithe of profits with community initiatives and to reaching out in other ways.

While this may smack of idealism thus far, over the last ten years, some 750 businesses in more than thirty countries have joined the movement. Most are small or medium sized businesses with a turnover of less than $20million annually. In some parts of Europe and in South America the EOC businesses have formed a network and co-operate in publishing promotional material. More than 200 EOC businesses are in South America and 300 in Europe. Some 100 are focused on agriculture, some 300 in the service sector, and the rest in manufacturing or related industries. In 1997, twenty-three German business people established an EOC Merchant Bank, dedicated to the development of EOC businesses in Eastern Europe, the Middle East and other parts of the world.

VALUE, VALUES AND CIVIC VALUE

Finally, I want to turn to the question of "measurement". It is, of course, when we address questions of determining the demonstrable value added that, in Christian action, and especially social and mission renewal, we can run into the deepest problems of terminology that I referred to at the outset.[55] However, I want to suggest here that the avoidance of measurement that some in the churches advocate is a flight from reason and justice as it is likely to complicate further our relationships with the secular (and increasingly the Christian) donor sphere.

In the UK a number of Christian bodies have withdrawn from academic "league tables" objecting that they do not "represent the fullness of education of the whole person".[56] Others have complained – having entered students who have "not done so well" – that "targets measure the wrong thing".[57] In some cases measurement in general has been condemned as mere "positivism".[58] These stances seem inadequate on at least three grounds.

Firstly, there is a moral communication issue. We may seek to articulate an idea of the common good which all people of reason may espouse but at the very moment that people of goodwill ask for some evidence of such warm intentions the Christian retreats too readily into the unknowability of all that we do. If it is a genuinely "*common*" good can it not be commonly quantified?

Secondly, a certain Christian tendency to conflate "measurement", "utilitarian immorality" and "market values" is intellectually dishonest. Our colleagues should be able to remind us that the history of accounting[59], along with the best of current developments in economics, offers us alternative vistas.[60] For example, current management accounting and audit methods are the product of negotiation, historical circumstance and the power of professions not tablets of stone uncritically binding on all institutions. Additionally, for all of its weaknesses in relation to issues related to population control, "Green" economics is developing new means by which to factor "future generations", "quality of life" and other seeming intangibles into the assessment of "value".[61] This is without mentioning the work of Mark Moore on "public value" and others on "blended value" and the "social return on investment".[62]

Instead of being caught in the wider ecclesial culture of complaint Christian innovators need to be at the forefront of conversations about who, what and how to "measure". We need to develop our own reasonable and reasoned matrices of value – let us call them "*civic value*".

One of the advantages of the "social silicon valley" model is that it allows "metrics" development to become one of the integrated but experimental features of the creation of new social institutions and innovations in which Christian principles are embedded. The "valley" becomes the accounting and economic laboratory in which new frameworks may be devised. And, once again, this presents the opportunity for rich inter-disciplinary conversation, common collaboration and witness in the public sphere just as current trends put such habits under the most pressure.

CONCLUSION

In this chapter I have drawn on a number of ongoing studies to begin to tease out a case for new strategies for mission and social action on the part of Christian institutions as we seek to work our way through tough economic times.

Influenced mostly by the UK and broader European context I suggested that we live in an increasingly fragmented culture – a new dark age. When such fragmentation is mixed with a lack of nuanced evidence on the part of the state and Christian churches, Christian responses to social need run an increasing risk of becoming fragmented themselves. They are also at risk of becoming depositories of excessive Christian hopes – or concerns.

In pursuit of a clearer identity I suggested that it is in a return to the rapidly evolving social sciences that much hope could be found – even by institutions that consider theology to have prior – or superior – disciplinary standing.

In order to renew a reasonable understanding of ourselves I have proposed a conscious culture of institutional disputation combined with new evidence gathering. I have also proposed the development of new common projects not least of which would be a series of "social silicon valleys". To address social need these would be structured centres where new institutions for dark times could be invented and scaled. They might best be co-located, at least in part, with our Christian schools.

As hubs of mission energy they could not save a national or established church but they could become the bases from which might emerge new institutions linking ideas, community and impact to support contemplation and preaching in their widest meanings. By combining disputation, common talk, shared research and common social risk-taking we would seek to make civic action a habit of the heart. In so doing we may just give rise to doubtless very different St Benedicts – or St Dominics – to challenge radically the increasing need that will soon be upon us.

NOTES

1   By "institution" I mean the full range of entities, works, congregations, agencies, associations, local Churches, Cathedrals, circuits and apostolates that members of mainstream Churches might embrace within their varying ecclesiologies broadly defined, the sum of which, I argue, is greater than "personal Christian beliefs".

2   These form part of ongoing research on the nature of leadership in faith-based organisations in European nations.

3   F. Davis, E. Paulhus, A. Bradstock (2008) *Moral, But No Compass – Church, Government and the Future of Welfare* (Matthew James: Chelmsford). For subsequent studies see F. Davis (2009) *Ideas, Institutions and Poverty Reduction in the EU: Questions for a Theology of Governance* in International Journal For Public Theology Vol 3, 1 (Leiden) and (forthcoming) F. Davis (2009) *Religion, Third Sector and Public Management* – special edition of The Journal of Public Money and Management (Routledge).

4 G. Davie (2002) *Europe: the Exceptional Case. Parameters of Faith in the Modern World,* (London: Darton, Longman and Todd).

5 F. Davis (2009) Religion, Third Sector, Policy and Public Management in *Public Money and Management* Vol 26, 6 (Routledge).

6 R. Gill (1998) *Theology and Sociology: A Reader* (especially chapter by Timothy Radcliffe OP) (Paulist Press).

7 This was the view of Michael Holman SJ, in his annual conference lecture to the Catholic Education Service in 2007. It is also present in G. Grace (2002) *Catholic Schools: Mission, Markets, Morality* (Routledge).

8 Of 35 interviewees in the UK 34 came from institutions where "community" was included in a mission statements, but all understood it differently.

9 A. Levine (2001) *Higher Education as a Mature Industry* in P. Altbach, P. Gumport, D.B. Johnstone (eds) In Defence of American Higher Education (Johns Hopkins).

10 See R. Plant (1999) *Socialism, Markets and End States* in J. Le Grand and S. Estrin (eds) Market Socialism (Clarendon).

11 See K. Mclaughlin, S. Osborne, E Fairlie (2002) (eds) New Public Management – Current Trends And Future Prospects (Routledge).

12 The example of "preaching" arises from an interviewee. For the commercialisation of spirituality see G. Lynch *Dreams of the Autonomous and Reflexive Self: the Religious Significance of Contemporary Lifestyle Media* in B. Spalek and A. Imtoual (eds) Religion, Spirituality and The Social Sciences (200) Policy Press.

13 The idea of a Christian education being a preparation for death comes from a former Headteacher at Ampleforth Abbey: see A. Howard (2006) Basil Hume: *The Monk Cardinal* (Headline*).* The "immensity of structural renewal" was noted in an interview in a university of part of an Order expressly committed to this aim.

14 This was the feedback from a leaders' workshop facilitated by academics from Warwick Business School for leaders of Christian institutions, May 2008.

15 And this is more than "managing as if faith mattered" as my friend, Helen Alford OP, discusses it in her book of that name.

16 Interview with institution head.

17 See A. Archer (1986) *The Two Catholic Churches – A Study in Oppression* and the discussion of "kingdom versus communion Church" in T. Radcliffe OP (2005) *What Is The Point of Being a Christian?* (Continuum).

18 There are several attempts to reframe the encounter with social sciences – but also to re-assess "secularisation" theory. For example, see B. Spalek and A. Amtoual (eds) (2008) *Religion, Spirituality and the Social Sciences – Challenging Marginalisation* and G. Davie (2007) *The Sociology of Religion* (Sage). Also G. Morgan (1997) *Images of Organisation* (Sage).

19 Workshop with Anglican Bishops; subsequent findings in *Moral, But No Compass* op. cit.

20 J. Stankeviciute, J. Rossiter and F. Davis (2008) *National Mapping of the Catholic Church's Work in Refugee, Migration and Asylum Rights* (Caritas Social Action/Von Hugel Institute).

21 "Revealed: The Modern Catholic" in *The Tablet* 19th and 26th July 2008.

22 R. Topping (2005) *St Augustine, Liberalism and The Defence of Liberal Education* in New Blackfriars 10:1111 (Blackwells).

23 In the UK the Secretary of State for Communities and Local Government has "lead" responsibility on these matters.

24 Harsh organisational conflicts were described by those advising the Bishops as "the NHS being the metaphor of the Good Samaritan" while the scale and purpose of the Christian voluntary sector had been under intense scrutiny during the passage of the UK 2006 Charity Act but had not registered in the core activity of the Bishops' Conference Secretariat.

25 See http://www.odi.org.uk/RAPID/Bibliographies/EBP/bibliography. html for a summary literature review.

26 from a theological distance – and many episcopal observations – Europe may look uniformly secular (but with Christian legacies) and yet most of the pioneering sociological studies in the region suggest a huge variety of secularisms at play that merit attention. In the UK we have been described as "believing without belonging" as while 71% of our citizens say they believe in a Christian God a little under 10% of them find their way to Church. This has been contrasted with a North European tendency to "belong without believing" leading some to suggest that religion in the UK is a "half way" case between the religiosity of the US and the barren lands of Scandanavia. However, these judgments may be affected by the structure and culture of the local state and its policymaking habits. It is ironic that despite an explicit commitment to *laicite* the French state is one of those most interested at the policy level in establishing which are the "acceptable" religious voices in society. Meanwhile I have argued elsewhere that the state's creation of social partnership councils, or "structured dialogue", in Europe can have more influence on theological authenticity – even of minority Christian communities – than any number of worthy papers, Episcopal utterances, Church going numbers or levels of Christian presence in national cabinets.

27 In three dioceses these were the priorities expressed and the social realities encountered in studies from 2005-07 by the Von Hugel Institute, Cambridge.

28 I am consciously using imagery here from A. Macintyre (2001) *After Virtue: A Study in Moral Theory* (Duckworth).

29 In this section I am drawing throughout on R. Plant and K Hoover (1991) *Conservative Capitalism in Britain and the US – A Critical*

Appraisal (Routledge); A. Denham(1996) *Think Tanks of the New Right* (Dartmouth); D Stone and A. Denham (2004) *Think Tank Traditions – Policy Analysis Across Nations* (Manchester) and interviews at various think tanks in Washington DC by the author (2005).

30   E.J Dionne (2004) *Why Americans Hate Politics* (Simon and Schuster).

31   R. Mishra (1977) *Society and Social Policy* (Macmillan).

32   For example, The Atlas Foundation.

33   Interview at Heritage Foundation (Dec 2004) and Acton Institute (2008).

34   See, for example, www.youngfoundation.org.uk and its global network.

35   A. Giddens (2004) *Beyond Left And Right – The Future of Radical Politics* (Polity Press).

36   Interview 2009.

37   See the sections on "Exit, Voice and Loyalty" in *Moral, But No Compass* op. cit.

38   The "Fresh Expressions" initiatives of dioceses of the Church of England that we visited as part of the *Moral, But No Compass* were "all local … all seeking to rebuild a local Church" and had much in common with earlier attempts by the Methodist Urban Theology Unit (www.utusheffield.org.uk) to make Churches more community focused.

39   "We cannot replace families, catechesis … or turn round a whole society" says one interviewee educational institution head (2008).

40   www.dur.ac.uk/st-johns.college/durham.ac.uk

41   For example, The Revd Brian Strevens founded the UK social enterprise of the year, The SCA Group; and The Revd Chris Beales (who went also to found the Inner Cities Religious Council under Mrs Thatcher's government) runs pioneering social enterprises generating revenues for Afghanistan.

42   The 1977 Housing (Homeless Persons) Act was taken through parliament by Stephen Ross MP with key advice from church-based groups.

43   S. Hopgood (2006) *Keepers Of The Flame: Understanding Amnesty International* (Cornell).

44   See www.youngfoundation.org.uk; also http://www.gsb.stanford. edu/csi/ and www.socialinnovationexchange.org and the Skoll Centre For Social Enterprise at Said Business School, Oxford. For a more passionate Christian take see A. Elliott (2006) 'The Spirit of Social Innovation,' a lecture for the International Futures Forum at the Scottish Parliament (www.internationalfuturesforum.com/iff-publications.php). Elliott is the former Moderator of the Church of Scotland and based currently at New College, Edinburgh University.

45   Even in the USA adequate provision for members of Religious Orders did not come from "within" but from the uncomfortable questions of

leading Catholic foundations "without". See M. J. Oates (1995) The Catholic Philanthropic Tradition in America (Indiana).

46 A key argument of *Moral, But No Compass* op. cit.

47 G. Mulgan, R. Ali, F. Davis et al (2006) *Social Silicon Valleys* (Young Foundation/British Council).

48 Interview (2008)Southampton University Health Innovation Unit.

49 The "constitutionalism" of the Dominicans as a contrast to the fragmentation of the Franciscans being a case in point. Even the anti-homelessness movement praised earlier encountered a series of striking "splits" as it grew from roots in the Society of St Dismas in Southampton.

50 B. Froehle and M Gautier (2003) *Global Catholicism – Portrait Of A World Church* (Orbis).

51 Based on interviews with philanthropists (2008) and the explicit comment from the Church of England Education Board that the "conundrum is the lack of compelling projects rather than a shortage of resources" (2008). See also studies in changing attitudes to Christian family philanthropy published by Foundations And Donors Interested in Catholic Activities www.fadica.org

52 See also: www.guardian.co.uk/commentisfree/belief/2009/feb/02/religion-catholicism

53 F. Davis (27 Jan 2007) Migrating Money in *The Tablet*.

54 F. Davis (23 Nov 2007) *The Government Borrows Another Great Catholic Idea* (*Catholic Herald*).

55 And yet respondents in Christian organisations often talk of a "value added" in a faith organisation that is absent from their "secular" counterparts.

56 Stonyhurst College in the period 2003-05 is a case in point as is Liverpool Hope University more recently.

57 A repeated reservation among interviewed Catholic teachers in our sample.

58 Archbishop Vincent Nichols, Chairman of the Catholic Education Services has expressed this view.

59 K. Hoskin (2005) Lecture on "*Leading or Horses – History and Management*" Warwick. See also http://www.wbs.ac.uk/faculty/members/keith/hoskin

60 Nobel Laureate Mohan Munasinghe is especially interesting on this point.

61 See, for example, P. Dasgupta (2001) *Human Well-Being and The Natural Environment* (Oxford).

62 M. Moore (1995) *Creating Public Value – Strategic Management in Government* (Harvard); Jed Emerson's work on www.blendedvalue.org and for social return on investment (SROI) see www.neweconomics.org

CHANGING THE CLIMATE: SPIRITUAL STEPS FOR SUSTAINABLE LIVING[1]

ABBOT CHRISTOPHER JAMISON OSB

Abbot, Worth Abbey.

INTRODUCTION

In this chapter, I hope to demonstrate that the monastic tradition can bring something to the debate surrounding two important and controversial problems: climate change and the dislocations that have happened in the world of finance. The two fields are clearly both areas where there is a vigorous public policy debate going on. Underlying public policy, however, are some fundamental ethical issues that are currently ignored in conversations about environmental matters and to some extent in conversations about the current economic crisis. The fundamental ways of thinking about both problems can benefit from a similar approach that draws on neglected truths about the human condition. Historically, the monasteries of Europe have been repositories of forgotten truths and neglected texts, enabling people to emerge from the Dark Ages and rebuild European culture. I will not make such grand claims for my insights in this chapter but I think that the insights of the Christian monastic tradition are still significant as we look to develop sustainable living.

Learning from the credit crunch

I begin with a cautionary tale about one of my forays outside the monastery to the City of London in 2003. My destination was the Financial Services Authority (FSA). With me was Roger Steare, a City consultant with whom I had just set up 'The Soul Gym', a project to promote ethical behaviour in business. In October 2002, the FSA had published a discussion paper entitled *An Ethical Framework for Financial Services*, an initiative strongly supported by the then Chairman of the

FSA, Howard Davies. In the foreword to that paper, Howard Davies notes that mechanical compliance with rules had done little to prevent problems in the financial sector and that this had serious consequences for a wide range of people. He continues with a statement that is chillingly relevant to our current financial crisis: 'the principles (of the FSA), our high level standards, are based on ethical values. But it is not clear that this ethos is fully understood or applied consistently by everyone working in the industry'. He continues '*An Ethical Framework for Financial Services* considers why that might be and how we might move beyond rhetoric and aspirational goals to have a tangible impact on firms' and individuals' motivation to do the "right thing".' The paper goes on to say that the FSA wants 'to establish a clear and explicit shared understanding about what integrity means in practice.' As a response to this, the Soul Gym was hired to carry forward that task and in 2003 we published *Integrity in Practice: An Introduction for Financial Services.* In simple terms, we offered virtue as the necessary ethical foundation for the financial services industry and showed how the four classical virtues of fortitude, justice, temperance and prudence provided a very practical basis for defining integrity. We asserted that to act in accordance with those virtues is to show integrity in practice and we gave illustrations from financial services to show this in operation. We concluded that the industry needed an ethical training programme alongside compliance training if it was to move beyond tick box compliance to achieve ethical integrity.

So what happened? To cut a long story short, Howard Davies retired as FSA chairman and the new Financial Services Skills Council took over responsibility for ethics. The ethical project ground to a halt and it would appear that we went back to concentrating on rule compliance. The window of opportunity was closed and five years later the consequences are clear. While there are many proximate causes of the current financial crisis, the ultimate cause is ethical. We can now see that the financial services industry was both over-regulated and unethical, a lethal combination, like a school with strict teachers where amazingly the pupils still get away with murder.

Quoting Howard Davies' prescient words again, the FSA has clearly failed to 'move beyond rhetoric and aspirational goals to have a tangible impact on firms' and individuals' motivation to do the "right thing".' This experience taught me that most people today are frightened of a serious engagement with ethics in the public forum. Popular ethics goes as follows: ethics at work is rule compliance; ethics in public matters is what the law allows; and the rest of ethics is labelled private. Public morality has become rule and law compliance so that public morality as morality no longer has a place in the public forum. The term 'moral' is now so debased that it is usually connected to 'moralising', a pejorative term to describe people sticking their noses into other people's business. As Howard Davies' warning in 2002 shows, however, this debasing of the moral sphere is the key to understanding the origins of our financial crisis.

THE METAPHYSICS OF CLIMATE CHANGE

Likewise, the debate about the physics of climate change must be accompanied by a debate about the metaphysics of climate change. We may well need rules and laws aimed at reducing climate change but they will not be enough. If we are to move beyond rhetoric and aspirational goals to have a tangible impact on people's motivation to do the right thing, then our culture will need to rediscover the reality of metaphysics.

Metaphysics can refer to a particular branch of philosophy but the word 'metaphysics' means literally 'what comes after the physics' and that is the meaning I am using in this chapter. I do not wish to debate the physics of the International Panel on Climate Change (the IPCC), though let me state clearly that I accept the conclusions contained in the summary of their 2007 report. However, as I have done with regard to the financial system, I wish to consider the question: when we've studied the IPCC's physics, what comes after the physics? Laws and codes are part of the answer but my aim is to explore what else we need in order to counter the environmental degradation that their report so clearly describes.

The first metaphysical port of call for a modern person facing a public issue is the human rights agenda. Most people today believe in human rights: they are the great metaphysical success of the modern era. Contemporary discussions about right and wrong usually revolve around human rights. So, for example, discussions about the end of life cluster around the right to die and discussions about gender cluster around women's rights. The development of human rights has succeeded in creating a framework within which to address many issues and the benefits have been enormous.

The human rights approach has, however, not provided a framework within which to address environmental issues. It has been noted for many years that there are human rights implications flowing from climate change, as people lose the means to live healthy lives in some countries. The human rights perspective helps us to measure the impact of climate change but it does not help us to remove its causes.[2]

Some people try to use the rights agenda by giving 'environmental rights' to the earth itself. A theological version of this involves a pantheist understanding of the earth as being not simply sacred but divine, mother earth as goddess. Some have claimed Christian tradition in support of such opinions. I believe, however, that Christian tradition does not support these views. I do accept the basic insight that the earth's ecology needs to be treated as a unity and that human well-being is part of that ecology. But that does not lead inevitably to earth rights or to pantheism. Those are not the only ways to approach the metaphysics of climate change. Moreover, such beliefs strike many people in this country as alien and strange, leading to caricatures that ecology is for tree huggers. In line with my thinking on problems within the financial sector of the economy, I believe that a much more robust metaphysical avenue is open to us – namely, the classical Christian tradition of the virtues. It is this tradition that St Benedict drew on in his Rule where he describes monks as 'people who delight in virtue'. The tradition of the virtues is weak in Britain but fortitude and justice, temperance and prudence are realities that still resonate positively in the lives of British people.

THE TRADITION OF THE VIRTUES

So how does the metaphysics of virtue work when applied to climate change? Let us take each of the four classical virtues in turn and look very briefly at their connection to environmental action. Firstly, fortitude: we are going to need courage to address our ecological problems. National and local communities will need courage to create a culture of environmental awareness and to take concrete steps to address climate change. Secondly, justice: justice will lead us to reach solutions that protect the weakest against the actions of the strong, so that third world countries are not left paying the ecological price for first world consumption. Thirdly, temperance: we will need to moderate our use of resources and develop technologies that enable us to use them more efficiently. Finally, prudence: we will need to act with prudence and not risk irreversible changes to the climate. At the same time, prudence requires us to recognise the benefits of industrial culture in relieving poverty, so we will not misuse the prudential principle to undermine those benefits. The key point to note, however, is that the tradition of the virtues insists that all the virtues are operative at the same time. So simply emphasising justice is inadequate: each virtue helps to define the other. As we shall see later, the addition of the theological virtues of faith, hope and love generates a comprehensive picture of human action that constitutes the Church's unique contribution.

These examples are broad applications of the virtues but even these generalised insights give the missing ingredient in the current environmental debate: the virtues provide an agreed framework within which to conduct the debate about what actions we need to take in the light of climate change. Most importantly, the framework of the virtues can be used for deciding both policy questions and lifestyle issues.

Public policy: nuclear power

So let me now give some worked examples in more detail. Firstly from the area of public policy, and here I purposely choose a controversial area of concern, namely, nuclear power generation. There is an important debate underway about the physics of nuclear power: for example, while changing hydrogen atoms into helium creates zero carbon emissions, the construction of the reactors requires enormous amounts of carbon generating activity as does the disposal of the radioactive waste product. Furthermore, the way to run a safe reactor needs careful calculation and risk assessment. After all those issues are resolved, the fact remains, however, that Britain cannot build enough reactors to meet all our energy needs and so they are at best part of a solution. But beyond that debate, a metaphysical question can be asked: are human beings capable of running a virtuous nuclear power industry? If a virtuous nuclear power industry is an oxymoron, then no matter what the physics, we should not have one. To be virtuous, the industry would have to have created a culture of people who are courageous, just, temperate and prudent. What might that look like? We need to have that discussion as part of the debate about nuclear power. The point I am making is that we need to discuss virtue as part of the public forum debate around all aspects of climate change mitigation.

Lifestyle: greed

So having looked at the culture of virtue and how it might apply to policy issues, let us now take a look at how virtue plays out in people's lifestyle and how that too is relevant to climate change. In this area, I choose as an example how the virtue of temperance can affect our lifestyle choices. We are increasingly aware that the Western lifestyle needs to change if we are to contain climate change. This is a problematic area because consumer culture is so embedded in our way of life, and of course this industrial system has brought real benefits. Too often people decry this culture's material impact without seeing its material benefits, so what has gone wrong with this commercial process? The danger lies not simply in what consumer culture has done to our bodies but in what it has done to our souls, which in turn has led to an abuse of the material world. In this area of life, the monastic tradition

162

offers some penetrating insights about temperance and about greed.

John Cassian was a great fourth century monk, the inspiration of St Benedict, and here is his account of greed in a monk. Greed is a work of the imagination that begins with apparently harmless thoughts. The monk begins to think that 'what is supplied in the monastery is inadequate and can hardly sustain a healthy and robust body.' The thought develops: 'the monk ponders how he can get hold of at least one penny.' When he has achieved that 'then he is distracted with the still more serious concern of what to buy with it and how he can double it' This in turn leads to disillusionment with the way things are in the monastery and the monk cannot put up with things any longer so he wants to leave the monastery.

What emerges from this and other monastic writings is how deeply seriously greed was taken by the founders of the monastic tradition. The two basic insights that they offer can be readily applied to the lives of ordinary people today. Firstly, greed has its origins in the mental picture we have of our life and its needs. Secondly, if we get that mental picture wrong, it is a potential source of disintegration in the lives not only of individuals but also of communities. Armed with those monastic insights about how greed actually works, we can now look at consumer culture.

Our Western culture is saturated with goods. The economically stable individuals and households who make up the majority of our population have more stuff than they actually need. While they might be persuaded to buy some more or different versions of what they already have, business recognises this material saturation and so the present thrust of consumerism is towards selling culture as well as things. Having saturated the world of our material needs, consumerism is now taking over our need for cultural goods such as music, entertainment and even moral purpose.

Let me give an example. Nike has a section of its website called 'Addicts Gallery' where runners can post comments like this from Raul: 'I am at the will of a higher purpose.' On the video clip accompanying it, we see Raul go running in Nike kit and then hear him say: 'I have plugged into a higher purpose, left this world and come back changed. I am addicted.' Even our souls are now consumerised and marketing is taking over not only our material imagination but also our spiritual imagination. So Nike and the other great corporations now inhabit our imagination, the place where greed is generated. Once planted there they can make us endlessly greedy, and that is exactly what they are doing.

Nowhere is this seen more clearly than at Christmas. The commercial world has taken over the popular imagination at Christmas and tells us that there are only two essential parts of the festival, namely, Christmas gifts and Christmas feasting. Shopping is the key to both these activities and over the shopping frenzy is laid a sentimental short cut to peace on earth: one day a year of peace and goodwill, then back to normal or rather forward to the sales.

An important bulwark against consumer Christmas is Advent. Advent is the traditional month of preparation before Christmas, a time of fasting and intense prayer, a time of eager expectation. It is above all a time to celebrate waiting as a normal part of human experience, when the Christian tradition invites us to wait for the birth of the Christ child. In Advent we rejoice that we are waiting, that there is still time to prepare a way for the Lord and we celebrate the virtue of patience. By contrast, the consumer world tells us not to wait but to 'buy now.' Greed cannot wait, so to learn to wait is a simple antidote to greed. Christmas has become greedy because Advent as a period of restraint and of waiting has disappeared.

Most people presume that Christmas begins when Christmas products appear in the shops in November. For example, a journalist who visited Worth Abbey a few days before Christmas was astonished to find no sign of Christmas decorations anywhere. She could not grasp that we were still celebrating Advent and that we would not start Christmas until the night of Christmas Eve. A credit card company once ran a Christmas campaign with the slogan: 'Access takes the waiting out of wanting.' By contrast, Advent puts the waiting back into wanting. Advent-with-Christmas has the potential to teach us how to enjoy the delight that comes from waiting.

Likewise the virtue of temperance is a key weapon in the fight against climate change. Is this just Puritanism? No, if Advent becomes a time of temperance, then the Christmas feast becomes a time of heightened enjoyment, both more restrained beforehand and more joyful on the day. Happy Christmas? Yes, provided we wait for it.

Happiness

The workings of temperance in order to contain greed is just one example of what virtue brings to people's lives as we learn how to reduce climate change. One of the most important insights of Catholic theology is that the life of virtue can be known by all, without reference to religious doctrine. This natural law approach means that the Church urges virtue on all people irrespective of their religious beliefs and wants to work collaboratively with all those who promote virtue. The term 'the good life' once meant the life of goodness and virtue that all decent people aspired to lead. This was seen as a life full of delight in living well; this was happiness, not a burden to be endured. This attitude is one that we must recapture if we are to find the human resources needed to cope with climate change.

It could well be that the current economic crisis and the growing ecological crisis act as a summons to rediscover this understanding of happiness. Our current culture describes happiness as feeling good and then adds that consumption is what keeps you feeling good. In other words, happiness is the same as pleasure. If, on the other hand, we identify happiness with knowing the good and doing good, then we have a happiness that does not demand endless pleasure and endless consumption. So what does it mean to know the good? It means knowing the goodness of creation, the goodness of other people and ultimately the goodness of God. What does it mean to do good? It means to live the virtues, responding generously to other people and working positively with others. Happiness is not feeling good, it is knowing the good and doing good. There is nothing inherently wrong with pleasure and consumption but if they are not set in the wider context of the good life then they will not make us happy. The climate is reminding our culture of forgotten truths.[3]

CLIMATE CHANGE AND THE EXERCISE OF VIRTUE

Speaking in 2001, Pope John Paul II said that 'Above all in our time, humanity has unhesitatingly devastated plains and valleys, polluted the waters, deformed the earth's habitats, made the air unbreathable, upset the hydro-geological and atmospheric conditions… It is necessary therefore to stimulate and sustain the 'ecological conversion' which over these last decades has made humanity more sensitive when facing the catastrophe towards which it is moving.'[4]

I believe that this ecological conversion involves individuals and society explicitly reaffirming that the classical virtues do indeed describe the good life. The churches in Britain, together with other religious communities, have a unique role to play in this regard. The four cardinal virtues have become endangered species, but the Church has given them sanctuary. They have been protected by the three theological virtues of faith, hope and love. For the Christian, the cardinal virtues are rooted in the theological virtues. Does this mean that only Christians have displayed fortitude and justice, temperance and prudence? No, because these virtues are part of being human. Nor does it mean that only Christians have thought like this. What this does mean, however, is that the Church is the principal global institution that sees in these virtues hard realities that have their own science that can be taught. In addition, the Church affirms them as an integral foursome that, when rooted in faith, hope and love, adds up to the heart of humanity. It is this totality of vision that is the Church's special contribution. As the great Catholic theologian Hans Urs von Baltahsar commented: 'The Christian is called to be the guardian of metaphysics in our time.'[5]

As the guardian of the tradition of the virtues, the Church, together with other religious communities, has a special role in this new and vital project. What will it look like? How will it come about? What can I do? It is the Church's task to take a lead in responding to those questions. There are to hand

166

various initiatives that offer practical examples of the virtues in action. For example, Transition Town initiatives are springing up, whereby over sixty towns work using groups of ordinary people looking at their local community to devise ways of being less oil dependent and emitting less carbon. There are initiatives of big business and very many other examples of virtuous action. For example, WS Atkins is a British based, multinational engineering and design consultancy. Their Chief Executive Keith Clarke recently said this: 'We cannot simply design a road, a building or a town, then ask key questions about energy use or environmental impact afterwards.' Atkins is developing a fundamental change of approach to designing capital projects, what they call Carbon Critical Design. They recognise that carbon trading is not the solution and they are seeking to make carbon credit an essential ingredient in all their work. Clarke concludes 'The time has come to move from worthy discussion about climate change to action. Only then will we begin to ask the questions that really matter, if we are to ensure that we, as professionals, show leadership in the most complex issue the world faces.'[6] The issue of climate change is creating an unusual convergence: local communities, major private sector businesses and the British government. Those who deny the human component of climate change are now simply being bypassed at every level.

VIRTUES AND THE FINANCIAL CRISIS

Climate change and the financial crisis both involve many layers of complexity. There are many problems which led indirectly or directly to problems in the banking system, for example. I do not wish to comment on those problems of an economic or technical nature. My key point is that the build-up of problems in the financial system would have been much attenuated if there had been greater exercise of the virtues I have described. If consumers had "waited" and not over-stretched in order to consume more; if borrowers had not lied when they applied for mortgages; if banks had not sold unsuitable products to vulnerable customers; if employees of investment banks had acted with greater prudence when developing and selling sophisticated financial instruments; and if senior banking employees had greater courage to call a halt to unsustainable activities, the history of the last few years would have been different. More generally, if the virtues were practised more widely, we would have a financial system that was more soundly grounded and sustainable. There are many contexts in which the virtues can be practised: in the higher realms of business, in our day-to-day transactions as consumers and savers, and within professional bodies, for example. It goes without saying that these virtues should be exercised by those who work within government and within regulatory systems as well.

CONCLUSION

In his magnificent work *After Virtue*, Alasdair Macintyre defends the tradition of the virtues and concludes that we are waiting for a new but very different St Benedict to re-express the virtuous life in our day. We are now fortunate in having a Pope who has self-consciously taken the name of Europe's great monastic patriarch and who is not afraid to challenge Western society's way of life. So let me leave you with the words Pope Benedict spoke in 2008, in reply to a priest's question about the environment: "In fact, it's not just a question of finding techniques that can prevent environmental harms, even if it's important to find alternative sources of energy and so on. But all this won't be enough if we ourselves don't find a new style of life, a discipline which is made up in part of renunciations: a discipline of recognition of others, to whom Creation belongs just as much as those of us who can make use of it more easily; a discipline of responsibility to the future for others and for ourselves. It's a question of responsibility before Our Lord who is our Judge, and as Judge our Redeemer, but nonetheless our Judge."[7]

NOTES

1 This is adapted from the text of the 2008 Operation Noah Lecture.
2 For example, the International Council on Human Rights Policy based in Geneva has published its first study of climate change only in 2008 under the title *Climate Change and Human Rights: A Rough Guide*. The title alone indicates how tentative this area still is.
3 cf. Jamison, C. *Finding Happiness: Monastic Steps for a Fulfilling Life* (London 2008).
4 Pope John Paul II, General Audience 17 January 2001.
5 *The Glory of the Lord (volume V): The Realm of Metaphysics in the Modern Age* p.656.
6 Clake, K., *The Carbon Critical Design Question* in *Angles* Issue 2: 2008.
7 Pope Benedict XVI addressing clergy in Brixen, Italy on 6 August 2008.

CHRISTIAN SOCIAL TEACHING – HOW SHOULD WE RESPOND TO THE CRASH?

PHILIP BOOTH

PRUDENCE – THE IMPORTANCE OF NOT SAYING TOO MUCH

Christian leaders have responded to the financial crash in various ways. Some notable figures have made wholesale denouncements of greed or called for more regulation or for completely new financial structures. Other commentary has emphasised the moral issues – a line that can best be summarised by the phrase 'a good world needs good people'. An early comment by Pope Benedict XVI, which others have echoed, suggested that the crash was a good time to reflect on the relative unimportance of material possessions.

This chapter discusses issues that might concern Christians as new developments in financial markets and regulation are debated over the coming years. Issues such as ethics in financial markets, over-consumption and debt, bankers' bonuses and the problem of usury have already been mentioned in earlier chapters and some of these are addressed again here. The role of the Christian commentator can be difficult when discussing these issues. Sometimes great discernment is required when coming to a judgment on technical economic points – indeed a definitive judgment on a particular issue is generally not possible. This leads to a legitimate question of what, if anything, Christians can bring to the discussion of the problems in financial markets.

This question has been dealt with in the Catholic Church in papal encyclicals and other documents. Most recently, Pope Benedict XVI commented in *Caritas in veritate* (10):

> The Church does not have technical solutions to offer and does not claim to interfere in any way in the

170

politics of States. She does, however, have a mission of truth to accomplish, in every time and circumstance, for a society that is attuned to man, to his dignity, to his vocation. Without truth, it is easy to fall into an empiricist and sceptical view of life, incapable of rising to the level of praxis because of a lack of interest in grasping the values – sometimes even the meanings – with which to judge and direct it.[1]

And John Paul II in *Centesimus annus* (43) wrote:

The Church has no models to present; models that are real and truly effective can only arise within the framework of different historical situations, through the efforts of all those who responsibly confront concrete problems in all their social, economic, political and cultural aspects, as these interact with one another. For such a task the Church offers her social teaching as an *indispensable and ideal orientation,* a teaching which, as already mentioned, recognises the positive value of the market and of enterprise, but which at the same time points out that these need to be oriented towards the common good.[2]

Thus there is a tradition in Catholic social teaching of identifying problems which might merit action and then leaving it to those knowledgeable in the field to debate, prudentially, what the best course of action would be.[3] In other words, "Of itself it does not belong to the Church, insofar as she is a religious and hierarchical community, to offer concrete solutions in the social, economic and political spheres for justice in the world. Her mission involves defending and promoting the dignity and fundamental rights of the human person."[4] Though there are groups of Christians that look for a specifically "Christian third way", this is not the general disposition of the Catholic Church or other mainstream Christian denominations.

Christian leaders should certainly regard it as legitimate to point out situations where they believe that it is possible that the economic order is not oriented towards the common good or is infected by human error (greed, materialism and so on). Christian economists might want to combine these insights with their understanding of economic theory, underlying economic principles and economic evidence to propose new ideas, policy and practice – and there will be debate about these policy issues. Rarely though will these ideas be grounded in objective Christian truth.

Economists can bring particular insights to the problems that are facing us. They are in a good position to make judgments about, for example, whether particular regulatory systems are likely to undermine ethical behaviour; whether particular tax systems will encourage risky behaviour and cause harm to specific groups in society; or whether there will be problems caused by interest rate caps (or the absence of interest rate caps) in consumer credit markets. But, even combining the work of economists, theologians, philosophers and others will not lead us to a specific *Christian* solution to the problems arising as a result of the banking crash. It will, though, help provide us with a framework of thinking – and hopefully some relevant empirical evidence – that will clarify our understanding in a way that is grounded in the reality of human nature. Christians can then make an important contribution to policy debates.

Perhaps Cardinal Pell of Sydney spoke wisely when he said: "The only thing we can say is to repeat the central teachings of Christ. When men and women over-reach themselves… trouble often follows… The financial crisis is enormously complicated, and I would hope that we don't attempt to say too much." Yes, there are important Christian perspectives on the financial crisis and the application of these perspectives can, no doubt, lead to better public policy for promoting the common good. However, we should proceed with humility and prudence – something that is characteristic of the earlier chapters of this book.

The 'common good'

Having mentioned the 'common good' it is important to define it. Increasing the common good is not about making society more equal, nor even making everybody better off. The common good has been defined in Catholic social teaching as "The sum total of social conditions which allow people, either as groups or individuals, to reach their fulfilment more fully and more easily" (Pontifical Council for Justice and Peace, 2005, 164). The importance of this would be broadly accepted by other Christians. We must not, however, assume that we can control and design political and economic systems in order to achieve the common good: indeed this is precisely the approach that has often led to squalor and oppression. We must also guard against assuming that the common good is something that can be measured: it is not possible in some utilitarian way to weigh up the increase or decrease in the common good that arises from reducing this or that tax for example. Different people will have different goals and callings and thus the phrase "*allow people to reach* their fulfilment more fully and more easily" is important. Promoting the common good is not necessarily about governments taking positive action as much as governments allowing the conditions to exist in which people can thrive and reach fulfilment. This principle will necessarily influence our consideration of specific issues below.

THE REGULATION OF THE FINANCIAL SYSTEM

Christian leaders have been at the forefront of calls for more financial regulation. The Archbishop of Canterbury, for example, suggested in March 2009 in an article in the *Guardian*:

> [G]overnments committed to deregulation and to the encouragement of speculation and high personal borrowing were elected repeatedly in Britain and the United States for a crucial couple of decades. Add to that the fact of warnings of some of the risks of poor

(or no) regulation, and we are left with the question of what it was that skewed the judgment of a whole society as well as of financial professionals.[5]

Several of the Archbishop of York's comments have certainly implied that he believed that participants in financial markets should be kept on a tighter rein. For example, he said: "To a bystander like me, those who made £190million deliberately underselling the shares of HBOS, in spite of its very strong capital base, and drove it into the bosom of Lloyds TSB Bank, are clearly bank robbers and asset strippers."

In March 2009, leaders of the major non-conformist churches called for increased regulation of financial markets, tax havens and more regulation surrounding accounting and reporting standards.[6]

We should be careful, as Christians, not simply to echo the cacophony of secular reactions. As has been noted, the over-arching principle as far as Christians are concerned is the "common good" – trying to ensure that the conditions exist to allow human flourishing. Just because the financial system has gone through a number of problems, it does not follow that regulating it more will facilitate the common good more effectively: this is especially so, of course, if many of the problems resulted from regulation in the first place. Catherine Cowley in her chapter is therefore right to take a step back and first ask whether parts of the financial system are orientated towards the enrichment of the few rather than society at large. The assertion that much banking activity does not benefit society as a whole is debatable, but it is valid to point to the possibility. The whole process of securitisation and the development of complex products, which Catherine Cowley blames for the crash, was approved not just by bankers but by central bankers, regulators and international financial "watchdogs" because it was believed that these products spread risk and reduced the cost of mortgage finance, including for the poor. Indeed, two huge mortgage finance 'warehouses' in the USA, Fannie Mae and Freddie Mac, were creatures of government, ultimately government backed and created for social policy reasons. But the fact that favourable views about modern developments in financial markets were widely held before the crash does not mean that the banking system, as currently constituted, serves the common good. How should we approach this subject as Christians?

One starting point is for Christians to ask themselves a series of questions that might establish a *prima facie* case that a particular matter is worthy of serious reflection and possibly policy action by government. The chapter by Townsend[7] in Spencer and Chaplin ed., (2009) discusses the sorts of criteria that Christians might use to make such a judgment. They start, as we have, with the proposition that the *raison d'être* of government action is the promotion of the common good. However, that does not mean that any government action we feel will make a society a better place is justified. Even changes to regulation that, on the basis of rational calculation, might appear to increase human welfare, might be seen as circumscribing the freedom of some and preventing them from promoting the common good. Furthermore, as Townsend points out, the Christian polity – and not government – is the primary mode by which God wishes to bring about the kingdom here on earth. Nevertheless, in creating the conditions for the common good, government does need to act in certain ways, argues Townsend. He reiterates the traditional Christian principles for legal action: governments should act to ensure that nobody is forced to do what is wrong or is prevented from participating in the promotion of the common good. This would imply, for example, that families' property and contracts must be protected from expropriation. As a parallel, Townsend also suggests that governments should respond to sins of omission. This would normally include ensuring that all had the basic necessities for dignified living, where the charity of fellow human beings omitted to provide for this. However, this might also include taking government action to prevent damage to the environment or, to take the case cited by the Archbishop of York, preventing people from rigging financial markets. Thus the Archbishop of York's argument may be justified on this ground, though it should be noted that rigging financial markets is already illegal and the short selling that the Archbishop criticised cannot really be said to have fallen into the category of rigging the market (see the chapter by Copeland in Booth ed., 2009).

Applying these theological constructs, Townsend himself suggests that the crisis calls for action at the moral rather than at the governmental level. He does suggest that there might be a case for preventing the granting of loans to those who obviously cannot repay them, and we will discuss this further below.

If we believe that there is a case to consider more regulation of the financial system based on these principles we then need to get into more detail and deal with the prudential aspects of the practical realities. For example, relating to financial regulation, we should ask whether problems in the financial sector arose as a result of a lack of regulation or, perhaps, too much regulation of the wrong type. Does the problem have an upstream cause which should be fixed first? Do the problems arise from a regulatory and legal system, as well as *ad hoc* government intervention, which prevent those working in the industry from being made financially accountable for their own decisions? Again, if this is so, the correct response might be to fix this problem, rather than to regulate the banking system to a greater degree. Finally, we can ask whether greater regulation will actually lead to more harm than good, knowing the imperfections that also pervade regulatory agencies.

These questions are essentially empirical economics questions about which theologians do not have any particular value to add in their role as theologians. The matters are also highly subjective. Different people will interpret the facts differently and come to different conclusions about how to act. Indeed, in the earlier chapters of this book we have seen Iain Allan and Catherine Cowley and Mick McAteer and Brian Griffiths come to different conclusions about regulatory issues relating to the behaviour of banks and also in relation to consumer credit.

On balance, it is difficult to make a *prima facie* case from a Christian point of view that there *must* be a regulatory response to the crash, except in one or two senses that will be discussed below. At the same time, a Christian cannot come to the view that increased regulation should be ruled out on theological grounds alone. There are areas where a regulatory response *might* be justified but whether to go forward and regulate in these areas is essentially a prudential judgment. In other words, there is a relatively wide field on which Christians of goodwill can conduct debate about these issues. This may seem like a long chain of reasoning to get to an inconsequential conclusion. However, it is an important conclusion. When ministers of religion, priests, and so on, use their authority to propose policy action in particular fields in which they lack the specialist knowledge to come to a wise prudential judgment they are in danger of undermining their authority in those areas where their voices should have special resonance. There is a big difference between an ordained minister or priest saying: "Recent events show that the financial system is not sufficiently tightly regulated" and him saying: "Recent events should cause us to ask whether existing regulatory structures serve the common good".

BAILOUTS

Christians will be instinctively concerned by the bailout of banks by the government. In an emergency situation, a bailout could be justified as being compatible with the common good. But, once that emergency is over, most Christians would want the government to take action to prevent such a situation arising again.

Arguably, there is a potential (or actual) injustice in a situation where the managers, owners and creditors of banks can obtain the benefits of success in good times but have their failures underwritten by taxpayers. Taxpayers then put their property at risk if the bank fails. Taking the income of future taxpayers in order to bailout banks is depriving the former of their property and may prevent them participating fully in the common good – especially if higher taxes lead to higher unemployment.

It is, of course, possible for a Christian economist to conclude, prudentially, that nothing can be done to improve on the current situation without damaging the common

177

good. He might argue that deposit insurance, a central bank providing lender of the last resort facilities, and government support for banks whose failure could bring the banking system down are a price we have to pay for a modern financial system from which everybody benefits. Other Christian economists might conclude that regulation is the solution to the problem in order to restrict the activities of banks. An alternative view is that there should be more effective legal mechanisms to make banks financially accountable for their mistakes so that 'bailouts' would no longer take place.[8]

So it can be seen that even those Christian economists who accept that action should be taken will not agree on what that action should be. Nevertheless, this is surely one of the most significant issues for Christians arising from the crash. It merits discussion not just because there are issues of economic efficiency arising from the moral hazard that is created by bailouts but, as Gregg notes in his chapter, because *moral* hazard involves the artificial encouragement of activity that is immoral and may lead to injustices. The problem of bank bailouts deserves explicit discussion amongst Christians, and in these terms.

THE PROVISION OF CREDIT

Is credit a Christian issue?

A number of authors in this book have commented that the availability of credit is one of the causes of the financial crash. It is interesting that the Archbishop of Canterbury also took up this theme in his Guardian article, saying: "A badly or inadequately regulated market is one in which no one is properly monitoring the scarcity of credit, and this absence of monitoring is especially attractive when governments depend for their electability on a steady expansion of spending power for their citizens." This was echoed by a number of other Anglican Bishops who, to a greater or lesser extent, blamed the government for being behind the increase in credit[9] including the Bishop of London who said:

We have been persuaded to believe it is possible to borrow our way into prosperity without self-discipline and sacrifice. Our addiction to borrowing has become inordinate and the deluge of communications from banks and others seeking to persuade us to take out fresh loans has contributed not a little to the crisis. It is becoming clearer how far we have been mortgaging our children's tomorrow to fund our today, both financially and in our use of the finite resources of the earth.[10]

There is no question that it is legitimate for Christians to raise the problem of credit as a potential public policy issue. Though it is not just a public policy issue – it is a moral issue too. Indeed, it is extraordinary how rarely the moral aspect of the subject is mentioned by clergy when giving pastoral advice to their flock.[11] The over-extension of credit may happen, of course, as a result of somebody finding themselves in very difficult circumstances, through no fault of their own. But, not withstanding this, indebtedness creates a potential situation of dependence on others and, in many cases, will imply an attachment to material goods. Pastors, perhaps, should discuss these issues more as problems of personal morality regardless of the wider economic and social consequences. Indeed, it can be argued that clergy have been remiss in not raising these issues until after the crash. Prudent behaviour, not becoming attached to material goods to such an extent that huge debts are incurred, and so on are virtues that should be cultivated at all times. Furthermore, good pastoral advice might also encourage saving – though not simply for the sake of accumulation. Saving reduces our reliance on others in old age, in the event of unemployment etc. Saving is also a discipline which, by its nature, requires us to *wait* for material goods. It also provides capital that enables an economy to thrive.

It could be argued that the desire for credit is part of a general desire for instant gratification in society which also manifests itself in binge drinking, obesity and casual sex. Waiting for the right context in which to have sexual intercourse, drink alcohol, eat, buy houses and consume goods are all decisions that have moral judgments at their heart.

179

Clergy cannot assume away commercial pressures in society, but they can encourage their flock to live lives of restraint and try to spread that virtue more widely. This is clearly an important area for Christians on which clergy and other Christians might comment, but perhaps the public policy aspects of the subject are the *least* important aspects.

Nevertheless, what might Christians contribute to the public policy debate? The Archbishop of Canterbury blamed the problems of credit expansion on a badly or inadequately regulated market and on governments wishing to expand the spending power of their citizens in order to be re-elected. However, probably the main factor in the expansion of credit was the loose monetary policy conducted by the US Federal Reserve Bank and by the UK Bank of England. It is difficult to argue that this was pursued – certainly in the UK – to make economic conditions more favourable to the re-election of governments. Indeed, arrangements making the Bank of England independent in 1997 were designed largely to prevent government using monetary policy to create a credit boom for political ends.

It is true also that many actions were taken by the US government to facilitate the extension of credit to the poor (see earlier chapters regarding the Community Reinvestment Act and the promotion of mortgage lending through Fannie Mae and Freddie Mac). I would certainly argue that this legislation was misguided. However, it should be said that those passing the legislation probably had, more or less, honourable intentions – specifically the intention of widening home ownership. These matters do merit comment; there may be a Christian aspect to them; however, as far as the government's role in creating credit is concerned, as has also been mentioned in earlier chapters, honest technical mistakes and lack of foresight may well have been the most important factors.

Related to consumer credit, of course, is the problem of usury. The Christian church has, throughout the ages, commented on the issue of usury. This teaching is formally documented in the Catholic church and therefore changes in the doctrine – or strictly speaking changes in the application of the doctrine – are relatively easy to follow (see Charles, 1998, Woods, 2005 and Gregg, 2007 for discussions of Catholic interpretations of usury, interest, credit and money). The chapter by Lilico also describes some of the more general history. Various interpretations of the concept of usury have applied at different times. These have included the charging of interest in any circumstances; the charging of interest when there is no sharing of risk by the lender; the charging of excessive interest to those who are vulnerable; and the charging of interest on the lending of money for which the lender has no use and which is not put to productive use by the borrower. The modern view on usury generally holds that that the charging of interest is not wrong in principle, especially where capital is put to productive use by the borrower. However, Christians may feel that loans that involve exploitation of somebody who is indebted, or consumer credit transactions which do not involve lending being put to productive use, are potential areas that may merit either voluntary restraint or legislative restrictions. As has been noted above, and also discussed by Lilico, it does not follow that, simply because Christians regard a particular form of behaviour to be wrong, there should necessarily be legislative prohibitions on that behaviour.

The regulation of credit

So, as with other issues, the regulation of credit is a prudential problem. It cannot be said that the tighter regulation of credit is a Christian imperative. Nor can it be said that having a deregulated credit market is a Christian imperative. The issues are similar to those discussed above in respect of financial regulation more generally: the aim should be the promotion of the common good. It is rather odd that the Archbishop of Canterbury should suggest that somebody should be monitoring the scarcity of credit as if one person – or a group of people – can somehow determine exactly how much credit there should be whilst having the foresight to know all the implications of any acts to reduce (or increase) the supply of credit. If there is to be regulation of the credit market in the name of the common good, then it should probably focus on well-defined problems where exploitation of some form may prevent persons from participating in the common good. But the hurdle for government intervention should be high. As Brian Griffiths pointed out in his chapter, the unintended consequences of regulation in this field are substantial – and Christians must take the possibility of unforeseen consequences of regulation into account: simply wishing improvements in the common good is not sufficient.

In this context, Charles (1998) points out the sheer difficulty of untangling financial transactions to find their ultimate purpose in modern financial markets. One example of this difficulty is given by new proposals from the UK Financial Services Authority (FSA).[12] These proposals may make lenders liable when borrowers cannot repay loans and also prevent mortgages being given when the mortgage is high relative to the value of the house and the income of the borrower. Making lenders liable for bad debts would move mortgage lending towards a *caveat vendor* position which could be dangerous given how easy it is for borrowers to hide their full circumstances from the lender. Lenders may then become reluctant to lend except at higher interest rates. Restricting the provision of mortgages on the basis of income and house valuations may well drive people to borrow in much more expensive unsecured consumer credit markets if they cannot secure borrowing on their house.

Thus, once again, the regulatory issues are tricky. There is no obvious Christian position and nor should there be so. Christians are perfectly entitled to have different views on these matters of regulation. But, Christians' views should coalesce more on the moral aspects of certain aspects of consumer credit. Both the morality of consumers over extending credit and the morality of sales people deliberately tempting individuals with offers of credit knowing that the potential debtor is already over-extended are matters on which Christian ministers should provide guidance, and they can do so with little fear that they are either straying from their area of competence or into subjective issues.

One area where the regulatory issues are certainly worthy of further consideration has been highlighted by Andrew Lilico. He discusses the problem of the granting of loans to people who cannot repay them – and his concerns are similar to those of Townsend. It might reasonably be asked, why any bank or other financial institution would grant a loan to somebody who was unable to repay it. But, as Lilico points out, somebody who already owes huge sums of money may borrow further money if the new lender has repayment priority upon being declared bankrupt. In effect, a bank making loans in this situation is depriving the earlier lenders of their property in the event of an individual becoming bankrupt. This could be regarded as unjust but also not in accordance with promoting the common good because there may be an incentive for banks to make loans that cannot be repaid with the arrangement involving the co-operation of the borrower. There are many ways of dealing with this problem. Direct regulation of consumer credit transactions is one way. A better way might be to make consumer credit contracts made in certain circumstances unenforceable if they undermine the rights of creditors with whom earlier arrangements have been made.

Debt and equity finance

Interestingly, the Archbishop of Canterbury, in his Guardian article also called for a "return to the primitive capitalist idea" of risk-sharing. The Archbishop's insight is important. Others have also pointed out that our monetary and credit system confuses savings with money and discourages people from taking risks with their savings.[13] This, in turn, means that debt finance tends to be more easily available to entrepreneurs than equity finance. If debt finance is more easily available than equity finance it raises the probability that a business will go bankrupt.

This is a key concern within the usury debate and equity finance is exempt from the prohibition on interest even within Islamic financial systems. The costs that arise from bankruptcy – both to the indebted and to those to whom money is owed – are of course enormous, and these costs are not just financial. This could be thought of as a purely moral matter, but there are public policy aspects too. As ever, these are matters for prudential judgment, about which Christians would disagree. It is, though, worth mentioning that the taxation system in nearly all developed countries strongly discourages equity finance and encourages debt. Perhaps this is something which, if it once served the common good (a doubtful proposition itself), no longer does so and should be the focus of policy action.

Government borrowing

It is interesting that Christian commentators seem to be much more sanguine about the problem of government borrowing than they are about private borrowing. Private borrowing is generally undertaken to allow people to spread their consumption over their lifetime – thus many of us borrow to buy a house. The effects are generally beneficial and benign though, as noted, there are problems of legitimate concern. Government borrowing, on the other hand, normally involves one whole generation outspending its income and imposing the burden of that on a future generation, without that future generation having any say in the matter. At times – for example, Japan in the current era and South American governments in earlier decades – such government borrowing imposes a burden on future generations that is potentially crippling and it is legitimate to ask whether EU governments and the US are going down that path today.

Most Christians would agree that there are legitimate reasons for government borrowing that do not raise public policy issues of a particularly Christian nature. For example, the government may wish to borrow during a period of temporary economic downturn or in emergencies such as wartime. However, the structural budget deficits of the UK, the rest of the EU, Japan and the US do not fall into those categories.

The problem of government borrowing certainly passes at least one of Townsend's tests of whether a subject might

184

be a legitimate area for public policy intervention. Future generations may be prevented from participating in the common good because of the burdens placed upon them by the current generation. As ever, this is not a black and white issue. It is something about which prudential judgment needs to be exercised. It is surprising, though, that there has been so little comment about the problem of structural budget deficits amongst all the concern expressed about private borrowing by Christians[14]. It is an issue about which a Christian perspective of the common good can be helpful, though never forgetting the complex underlying technical issues that must also be considered when deciding on specific policy action.

'NEW' FINANCIAL INSTITUTIONS AND CHRISTIAN SOCIAL MOVEMENTS

Christian social action is not primarily about changing public policy. There is a long history, in all Christian denominations, of Christian social movements in the fields of health, education and also in financial and insurance services. These social movements do not only serve Christians and they may or may not be based around profit-making institutions. A number of previous chapters discussed such institutions and movements explicitly. They were also discussed in Pope Benedict's encyclical *Caritas in veritate*[15]. Credit unions are perhaps the best-known current example of financial institutions with a Christian foundation that lie outside the mainstream proprietary sector.

Professor Stefano Zamagni[16] has summarised very effectively what lies at the heart of these institutions of civil society. The institutions promote wellbeing – not just material wellbeing – but are not profit maximising proprietary firms. Profit maximising institutions in the market economy have contractual obligations as their *modus operandi* – for example, I take out a loan from a bank, I then repay the loan with interest. Charitable organisations have love at their heart – we do charitable acts expecting nothing in return. Governmental action has coercion at its heart – if I do not pay my taxes I go to prison. On the other hand, the institutions of civil society have reciprocity at their heart – individuals and communities perform acts for each other without contractual obligations, altruism or coercion defining all aspects of those actions. This is the basis of friendly societies, mutual building societies and credit unions many of which have been important in UK financial markets at different times.

In the financial sector, the economic issues surrounding such institutions can be complex. Sometimes there will be an aspect of charity – people give their time to the management of credit unions freely, for example. Sometimes, the institution will make some profits and its employees will be paid but it will have a particular ethos: perhaps it will prefer to remain small and rooted in the community. Because trust is so important in ensuring that the financial system functions properly, there will often be significant economic benefits from institutions where supporters and members have a common bond and a sense of trust between them, though this can limit their size. In general, it can be difficult to distinguish between the exercise of Christian fraternity, charity and self interest in such organisations. However, it is not necessary to make such distinctions as these financial institutions arise to meet human need – whether they are primarily motivated by charity, fraternity or self interest, or some combination, is beside the point.

It is interesting that there is much agreement from Christian commentators on economic matters about the importance of these institutions of civil society. Many Christian socialists favour them. As has been noted, these institutions were explicitly mentioned in *Caritas in veritate*. They also find favour with supporters of a free economy. Furthermore, the Christian distributist movement particularly favours them, arguing that market economies lead inexorably to large uncompetitive firms crowding out social movements and that of institutions of civil society can provide financial and other services.

There is little empirical evidence in support of this distributist position. Proponents of a free economy recognise that a free economy does not just involve profit-maximising business corporations acting within markets. In our free economic and social lives, we can interact with a huge range of institutions with a wide range of different objectives and motivations. Whilst there are technical reasons why firms have grown bigger and have thus have been more likely to use the proprietary form of organisation, some of the institutions of civil society (particularly in the insurance field) have disappeared simply because the government has taken over their function. Friendly societies, for example, arose because they were effective at monitoring and helping claimants in the mass provision of health, unemployment and disability insurance. In addition, serious research suggests that the hugely increased level of financial regulation in recent decades also played a major part in making our financial scene look more uniform. In the days before regulation and government guarantees for financial institutions, they had to demonstrate to those using them that they were 'sound'. They no longer have to do so. Before pervasive financial regulation, financial institutions therefore often remained relatively small, rooted in the community and owned by their member-customers. Life insurance companies were often owned by their policyholders, as some still are, as a way to avoid conflicts of interest between owners and policyholders: these conflicts are now managed by statutory regulation. Thus, the institutions of civil society often performed a function – signalling trust and reliability – that has been taken over by regulation. In addition, the increased volume of regulation also makes it more difficult for new entrants to come into the market and compete with the existing giants – there are huge economies of scale in the costs of complying with the literally thousands of pages of Financial Services Authority (FSA) regulation. Of course, large institutions have, as has been noted in a number of other chapters, been given additional implicit guarantees by the state that smaller institutions do not get. This is a serious impediment to smaller competitors.

Others would disagree with the above analysis and suggest that smaller, credit making institutions should be explicitly encouraged and tightly regulated.

Nevertheless, it is true that more institutional variety within the financial sector may well better meet human needs – and not just financial and material needs – within the context of a free economy. In his chapter, Francis Davis calls for a renewal of Christian social entrepreneurship which itself is necessary to make Christian institutions of civil society flourish again. But we do have to consider the political, legal and regulatory framework that will allow such organisations to thrive. Once again, Christians will disagree on such matters; there is no theological answer to the question "why have the institutions of civil society degraded?" However, Christians should be concerned by their degradation and Christian economists should contribute to the debate about their reinvigoration. Christian economists' perspectives can complement philosophical and anthropological observations about the importance of the institutions of a civil society and might help us understand how they can once again be nurtured. It is worth noting in passing that, if there were a renewal of civil society and non-profit-maximising institutions in the financial sector, then this would be in the context of increased concern being expressed by Christian leaders about interference by government in charities, Christian schools and other voluntary organisations. In other areas, institutions of civil society are under attack.

IN CONCLUSION – THE CRASH AND ETHICAL ISSUES

Christian social teaching is not Christian political teaching or Christian economic teaching. There is a strong ethical dimension too. Indeed, in two of his first three encyclicals, Pope Benedict XVI has stressed the necessity for all social action to have the correct moral orientation. In this context, many of the chapters of this book – especially those by Iain Allan, Samuel Gregg, Archbishop Vincent Nichols and Abbot Christopher Jamison – have dealt at length with ethical problems. Two of those chapters have asked whether a focus on regulation, and ticking regulatory boxes, has crowded out a perceived need to use ethical judgement. These ethical issues are of crucial importance in our response to the crash as Christians.

Arguably, ethical failings were not the main cause of the crash – though they may have been one of many contributory factors. It is also likely that ethical compasses were severely distorted by the perception of government bailouts and certain aspects of regulation[17]. But, there is a sense in which none of this matters. Ethical behaviour should not just be reserved for occasions when we think it will have a profound impact on the success of the financial system. Every "liar loan", every transaction undertaken by a trader in his own interest, rather than in his company's interest, every loan that is "oversold" to a consumer who cannot afford to repay it, and so on, has its effects on others. Furthermore, a breakdown in trust amongst those working within the financial system seriously degrades its operations. Economists have something to contribute to the debate as to how systems of regulation can reinforce or undermine ethical behaviour. They have also something to contribute to an understanding of how ethical behaviour can increase efficiency in markets and wellbeing in society as a whole – though that is not the prime reason for behaving ethically, of course. But, aside from these observations, this is an area where the economists should perhaps sit back and allow the theologians and Christian philosophers to take the prominent role in the debate.

At the same time, perhaps theologians and Christian ministers should take a less prominent role in making judgements about the political economy responses to the crash. There are certainly aspects of government policy which have a moral aspect and on which theological reflection can be useful. But, in general, if the goal is a higher standard of behaviour, government regulation is the wrong instrument. Immorality requires a change of heart not a change in the law. If immorality and unethical behaviour abounds, one cannot assume it will not pervade regulatory bureaus. It is certainly a mistake to have, as a default position, the view that more regulation is the answer to problems in financial markets – human institutions cannot be perfected by giving power to other human institutions.

Christians generally, will argue that the particular policy responses to the crash are matters reserved for prudential judgement: two Christians of goodwill could legitimately disagree about the appropriate action to be taken. This chapter has distilled some issues that are of particular concern to Christians and has provided some thoughts about the criteria that might be used to make policy judgements. It is important that we have a public policy framework that works with the grain of human nature so that, when making ethical judgments, we are not pushing water uphill. The policy framework must, of course, promote the common good – that is, as far as it can, allow human flourishing. It is also important that we recognise the limitations of public policy in terms of its ability to perfect the world.

NOTES

1 http://www.vatican.va/holy_father/benedict_xvi/encyclicals/documents/hf_ben-xvi_enc_20090629_caritas-in-veritate_en.html
2 http://www.vatican.va/edocs/ENG0214/_P6.HTM
3 With all Christians, of course, not necessarily being on the same side of the debate!
4 Justicia in mundo, World Synod of Bishops, 1971, 37.
5 http://www.archbishopofcanterbury.org/2324# accessed 9 October, 2009.
6 http://www.standrewsurcsheffield.org.uk/node/329
7 Government and social infrastructure.
8 The author's own position.
9 See: http://news.bbc.co.uk/1/hi/uk/7801667.stm
10 See: http://www.telegraph.co.uk/news/uknews/4015946/Gordon-Brown-dealt-fresh-blow-as-Bishop-of-London-criticises-false-financial-hopes.html
11 US churches and some of the evangelical churches in the UK are exceptions.
12 See: http://www.fsa.gov.uk/pubs/discussion/dp09_03.pdf
13 This is the basic position of the Austrian school of economics.
14 Interestingly, Archbishop Rowan Williams did criticise increases in borrowing caused by the recession but not the structural deficit, but he is one of the few people to have mentioned the issue at all.
15 Especially in section 3.
16 Zamagni advised the Pope during the writing of the encyclical and probably particularly influenced section 3.
17 See "Ethics alone will not prevent financial crises", Philip Booth, *Financial Times*, 12 November, 2009: http://www.ft.com/cms/s/0/49310344-cfb6-11de-a36d-00144feabdc0.html